Miss Droese

Indian gems for the master's crown

From bondage to freedom

Miss Droese

Indian gems for the master's crown
From bondage to freedom

ISBN/EAN: 9783337269135

Printed in Europe, USA, Canada, Australia, Japan

Cover: Foto ©ninafisch / pixelio.de

More available books at **www.hansebooks.com**

INDIAN GEMS FOR THE MASTER'S CROWN

I. THE INDIAN DEVOTEE AND HIS DISCIPLES
II. FROM BONDAGE TO FREEDOM; OR, THE LIFE OF TULSI PAUL

BY MISS DROESE
OF LANDOUR, INDIA

With Illustrations

LONDON
THE RELIGIOUS TRACT SOCIETY
56 PATERNOSTER ROW, 65 ST. PAUL'S CHURCHYARD
AND 164 PICCADILLY
1892

CONTENTS.

I.—THE INDIAN DEVOTEE, AND HIS DISCIPLES.

CHAP.		PAGE
	Prefatory Note,	11
I.	A Strange Visitor,	13
II.	The Faqír begins his Mission,	20
III.	The Catechist visits Phulkiya,	24
IV.	The Missionary visits Phulkiya, and so does the Faqír,	31
V.	The Widow Bhaktin,	35
VI.	The Clouds begin to Gather,	40
VII.	The Storm Breaks,	48
VIII.	The Pamphlet and its Story,	52
IX.	A Step onwards,	58
X.	Bhaktin turned adrift by her Brother,	65
XI.	Jethú's Wife brought to the Lord,	71
XII.	The Lord manifests His Power,	76
XIII.	The Lord's Way made Manifest,	80
XIV.	The Day of Trial and the Day of Blessing,	86
XV.	'Blessed are the Dead which die in the Lord,'	91

CHAP.		PAGE
XVI.	The Seeds of Caste still linger,	96
XVII.	Bhaktin learns to read her Bible,	101
XVIII.	Tulsiya's Husband visits Phulkiya,	106
XIX.	The Meeting of Father and Son,	111
XX.	The Power of Christian Love,	119
XXI.	The Triumph of Faith,	127

II.—FROM BONDAGE TO FREEDOM; OR; THE LIFE OF TULSI PAUL.

	Prefatory Note,	135
I.	Tulsi Paul's Wedding and his Studies,	137
II.	Some Phases of Idolatry,	147
III.	First Contact with Christians,	153
IV.	Spiritual Conflict,	158
V.	The Lord Jesus gains the Victory,	162
VI.	Tulsi Paul preaches Christ,	165
VII.	Tulsi Paul's Great Trial,	170
VIII.	Tulsi Paul's Work as Pastor,	175
IX.	Tulsi Paul's Disciples, and his Preaching Tours,	182
X.	Tulsi Paul's Last Years and Death,	190

LIST OF ILLUSTRATIONS.

	PAGE
An Indian Village,	*Frontispiece*
A Faqír,	15
Native Christians Preaching in a Bazaar,	25
Hindu Village Council,	45
Women's Jewels,	67
Native Boat,	118
Bullock-Cart,	122
Tulsi Paul,	134
Brahmin at Prayer,	139
Hindu Faqír,	146
Hindus Bathing in the Ganges,	149
Indian Jugglers,	183

I.

THE INDIAN DEVOTEE
AND
HIS DISCIPLES

𝔄 True Story of 𝔐issionary 𝔚ork in India

Translated from Hindustani and Revised by the
Rev. J. P. ELLWOOD, C.M.S.

PREFATORY NOTE.

THE following narrative is perfectly true, and the characters depicted so faithfully were all real characters, and the events occurred as recorded by the writer. The lady described as the missionary's daughter is Miss Droese, the writer, and the missionary was her father, the Rev. E. Droese, who for forty years laboured for the Lord in India, and who before the close of his life translated the Scriptures for the Pahàris. Living on the hills not far from Phulkiya, Miss Droese knew personally all the characters she describes, and the conversations said to have taken place on several occasions were all reported to her, or she was present on the occasion. In speaking of this story, soon after my arrival in England, I was asked by a lady if it was true, and if all the facts could be proved; 'for this is the kind of story,' she said, 'we require.' I was happy to be able to reply that the writer had stated nothing but what was perfectly true.

The object of the writer, in putting forth this story of real life originally, was to instruct and interest the native Christians of India in the conversion of the villagers to Christ, but her object in wishing to put it before the English public is a little different. She wishes to interest and instruct, but in a different way. The story has been translated into several foreign languages, and all who have read it say how simply it puts before the European the difficulties and trials of men in the East who wish to become Christians, and how much more real it makes missionary work and its difficulties.

There is, however, another way of looking at this

story. It furnishes an example of the way Christianity will probably spread in India, if we are not very careful to train our Christians well, and follow up the work we have already begun in many large centres. Brahmoism is an example how very near a religion may be to Christianity, and yet how very far from it in real Christian teaching. The Missionary Societies and the Christian Church in India will find that now and then a sect will arise embodying the chief tenets of Christianity, whilst rejecting its practical confession before the world, and setting aside just those points which distinguish it from every other religion, and putting forth these doctrines as philosophical speculations, to be received as pious opinions and probable truths. The following quotation from *Word, Work, and Will*, by the late Archbishop Thomson, will not be out of place :—' For there is a danger, to which perhaps we are not sufficiently alive, not so much of a still rejection of Christianity, as of the foundation of spurious and adulterated beliefs, in which some Christian elements are adopted, mixed with a large leaven of old superstitions, that hang still about the religious consciousness of the people, and are difficult to uproot. The history of the first century, with its Ebionite and Gnostic extravagances, will have been examined in vain, if we cannot see how easily those phenomena might repeat themselves with Buddhist and Brahmin, and even the Maori or the Kaffir.'

This narrative throws light on the same subject, and will furnish the Church with the way this takes place, and how it may be dealt with when it arises. In commending this little volume to our readers, we ask them to remember the Christians of Phulkiya in their prayers.

CHAPTER I.

A STRANGE VISITOR.

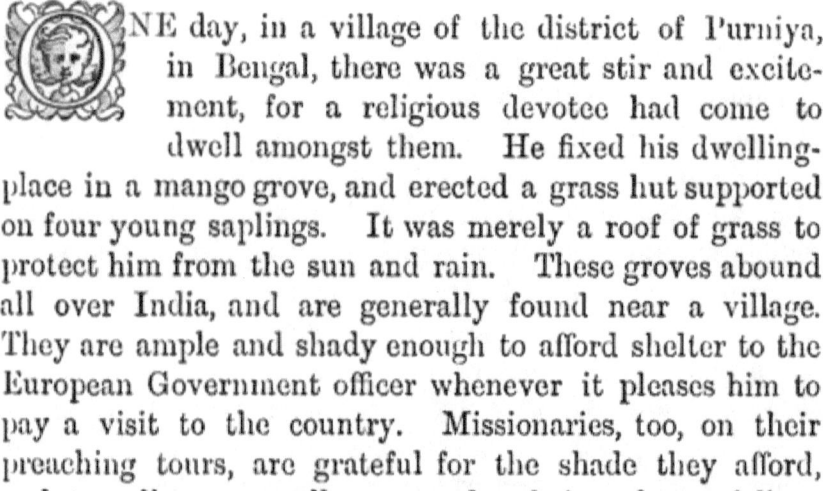NE day, in a village of the district of Purniya, in Bengal, there was a great stir and excitement, for a religious devotee had come to dwell amongst them. He fixed his dwelling-place in a mango grove, and erected a grass hut supported on four young saplings. It was merely a roof of grass to protect him from the sun and rain. These groves abound all over India, and are generally found near a village. They are ample and shady enough to afford shelter to the European Government officer whenever it pleases him to pay a visit to the country. Missionaries, too, on their preaching tours, are grateful for the shade they afford, and travellers generally rest under their welcome foliage during the heat of the day.

Wandering and religious devotees in India are commonly known by the title of *Bábá-Ji*, *Bairági*, or *Faqír*, but the two former are chiefly appellations in use amongst the Hindus, whilst the latter is decidedly a Mohammedan title. They are often, however, intermixed, and used in common for any religious devotee who fasts and prays, and wanders about the country begging his bread. Amongst the common people they are very much reverenced, and the presence of one of them in a village is supposed to augur well for the religious and temporal welfare of the people. No wonder, then, when it was announced in the village that a Bábá-Jí had come to remain with them for a time, that all the people, great and small, ran out to see him, to give him their salutation, and pay their respects to one so holy.

The appearance and bearing of the Bábá-Jí, or religious devotee, was most peculiar. He looked morose, sat like a statue, and appeared to take no notice of the people who came to see him. Opposite his hut he made four fires, placing one at each corner of a square, in the centre of which he sat, staring into the fire. He now and then cried with a loud voice and said, 'I know the true way of salvation; I have the true knowledge of salvation.' After delivering himself in this way, he remained silent. No one asked him what he meant by this declaration; but the villagers brought him milk, curds, and food, and placed them before him. Yet he would not eat; he merely said gruffly, 'I do not want your food; my religious merit is my food;' and, indeed, no one ever saw him eating. Beneath his grass hut there were two or three dirty earthen vessels covered over, but they did not appear to be of any use. When the people saw that he would not take their food, they brought him rupees and pice— Indian money—and these he accepted most willingly and religiously.

Now it came to pass that the people of another village at some distance heard the wonderful story of the Bábá-Jí, for news of this kind travels quick in India, and seven of them came to see him. On hearing him cry as usual, 'I have the true knowledge of salvation,' they said to

A FAQIR.

him, 'Bábá-Jí, can we obtain this true knowledge of salvation?'

The devotee was some time in giving an answer. He first stirred the burning embers around him, and then, having turned to the questioner, said, in a cold, indifferent tone, 'If you are willing to fast seven days and seven nights, then I will tell you the secret how you may attain to that better world.'

After a little deliberation these seven men agreed to fast for seven days and seven nights, as the Bábá-Jí desired. They saluted him, according to the custom of the country, took their leave, and set out home again. On the second day, however, two of them failed to carry out their resolution, and broke their fast. After five days other two did the same. Three did indeed keep their fast, but one of them was so weak from the effects of it that he was unable to leave his bed. Thus, of the seven men, only two set out to the hut of the devotee. On the way they met a milkwoman carrying milk and curds in her vessels. One of these poor men, worn out and famishing, fell to the ground as he saw her, and cried out, 'I cannot endure any longer! The Bábá-Jí's hut is a long way off, and I have not the strength to carry me there: why should I not drink some of this milk, and save my life? for surely I shall die on the road without finding the true way of salvation; so what does it matter? Here, old woman,' said he, 'give me a half-pice worth of milk.'

His companion tried to dissuade him, and said, 'Why will you lose your soul? our desire is near completion.' But he would not listen. He drank the milk, and returned home. There was now only one left, and he continued his journey; but the pangs of hunger and thirst were very great, and he was so weak that he could only go stumbling along a few paces at a time. At last he reached the hut of the Bábá-Jí, and falling on his face before him said, 'Bábá-Jí, be pleased to tell me now the secret of the way of salvation.'

To outward appearance, the devotee did not seem particularly pleased to see him.[1] He asked, in a heartless and careless way, where the six other men were. The man replied, 'They have broken their promise, and I have come alone. I have kept the fast for seven days and seven nights, and have touched neither food nor water. Give me now the information you promised, and for which I have fasted so long.' On hearing this, the countenance of the Bábá-Jí displayed signs of a kindly feeling. He made the man take a solemn oath that he had indeed fasted the appointed time, and pointing to one of the old covered smoky-looking vessels, said in a cold manner, 'There it is; take it, and value your prize.'

The poor perplexed cultivator looked here and there, and becoming confused, exclaimed, 'What shall I take? There is nothing here but some old earthen vessels.' The devotee replied, 'Take off the lid from that vessel, and in it you will find the secret of the true knowledge of salvation.' All trembling, the man quickly took off the lid, and to his consternation only found a torn tract or pamphlet. When he had seen what it was, he thought in his mind, 'Surely the Bábá-Jí has been playing a trick on me, and deceiving me.' He gave vent to his feelings, and cried out in a distressed voice, at the same time holding the tract in his hand, 'Of what good is this to me?'

When the devotee saw his excitement, he was very much pleased, and said, 'Do not trouble yourself, unneces-

---

[1] It is considered a sign of great sanctity to subdue all exhibition of feeling.

sarily, brother; take the tract home and read it carefully, and then you will ascertain the true knowledge of salvation.' The man seemed somewhat comforted by this assurance, and kept looking at the pamphlet for a long time. He then wrapped it up carefully in his shawl (a kind of cloth used to cover the shoulders, and made of cotton), and having fallen at the feet of his spiritual guide he did obeisance, and returned to his home. In his excitement he altogether forgot his hunger, thirst, and weakness, and said in his heart, 'This piece of paper has given me new life and new hope. I feel very happy.'

On reaching home he read the tract over and over again, and weighed well its teaching; for he was truly desirous of realising its meaning. After some days it came into his heart to pay another visit to the Bábá-Jí, and become his disciple. When he reached the mango grove near the village, the devotee was not there, for he had left the place. The people said he went away on the very day he gave the piece of paper to the cultivator. No one knew whence he had come, and no one could say whither he had gone.

The cultivator returned home, but he had no heart for anything, so much had his soul been stirred by the contents of the little tract. He could not give his mind to anything else, nor find rest in any worldly occupation; his work became distasteful to him. At last he gave up his land, family, home, and everything, and putting on the garb of a religious devotee, he became a Faqír. He travelled over the whole country, preaching and making known this new religion, the knowledge of which he had found in that remarkable tract or pamphlet.

CHAPTER II.

THE FAQÍR BEGINS HIS MISSION.

THE teaching of the pamphlet, which made such an impression on the mind of the cultivator, was as follows:—The Hindus were enjoined to give up the worship of idols, and to serve the one living and true God, who made heaven and earth. They were told that the Hindu gods and incarnations could not save mankind; the true Incarnation only could save man—the Lord Jesus Christ, who was born of a pure virgin, without sin, and gave His life to save mankind, that whosoever believeth on Him should have everlasting life. All were recommended to put themselves under the protection of the true Incarnation.

This eager disciple of the Bábá-Jí, as we have observed in the previous chapter, now assumed the garb of a religious devotee or Faqír. He had never seen a missionary, nor any Christians. He did not know even of their existence. He knew nothing but the contents of his tract. He was very anxious that others also should accept this religion, and proclaimed the teaching of this torn tract with so much earnestness and zeal, that wherever he went the people gathered in crowds to hear him, and listened with heart and soul to his words. Very many people became his disciples, and, having given up idol-worship, began to pray to the Lord Jesus Christ and the Bábá-Jí.

This Faqír or devotee, as we shall now call the poor cultivator, in order to distinguish him from the Bábá-Jí, gave the name of *Satya-Gurú*—namely, true spiritual guide and teacher—to Jesus Christ, and instructed his disciples to call him also *Satgurú*—true teacher. Since then his followers have always been called *Satguruwás*—followers of the true teacher.

The Faqír, or Satgurú, instructed his disciples to remain firm in this new religion, and not to allow any one to lead them astray, or frighten them into forsaking it. He often tried in various ways to prove the strength of their faith, and test the sincerity of their devotion. To one he would give an order like the following: 'You go into that lake, which is full of alligators, and stand there for two hours, and put your trust in the Lord Jesus Christ, fully believing that He will not allow them to drag you down and eat you. By doing this, it will be seen whether you are a true servant of God or not.' To another he would say, 'You go at midnight to a certain jungle, or mountain, and, having gathered a *maund* of wood' (that is, eighty pounds), 'burn it on the spot; and when it is all reduced to ashes, plant this stick on the top of the ashes, and come back again. If you have faith, then tigers and bears will not be able to harm you.'

It is very wonderful that his disciples were so simple-minded and ingenuous as to allow their faith to be tried by such means; but the truth is, they firmly believed in and obeyed their teacher, and held him in great reverence.

The Faqír did not settle down in any fixed place, but went round every year, and visited his disciples at their own homes, staying a week or so in each place, and receiving from them such gifts as are always offered to a religious teacher; for every native of India is taught from early childhood thus to provide for his spiritual guide. Wherever there were two or three disciples in a village, he appointed one of them as their guide and teacher. He ordered them to make a careful copy of his pamphlet, to meet together every Sunday to read the pamphlet before the people, sing *bhajans* or hymns, and in this way worship the true Incarnation, Jesus Christ.

In the villages of Tirhút, Purniya, and Sáhibganj, on the banks of the Ganges, many people became the disciples of the Faqír and devotee. When the Brahmins saw that the new religion was spreading, and that their revenue on this account was steadily decreasing, they began to be much exercised in mind about it, and laid plans for bringing back the people to their allegiance. They held a council amongst themselves, and laid heavy fines on the people, and commanded them to return to the worship of idols, and call upon the heathen gods as before. But the disciples of the Faqír were not afraid of any threats; for they neither paid any fine nor attempted to appease the Brahmins in any way. Then the Brahmins became their open enemies, and put them out of caste, and began to persecute and trouble them in every way; and this was carried to such an extent, that in three or four years many of the followers of the Faqír deserted his teaching and doctrine, and fell back into their old habits of life. In the village of Phulkiya there were once one hundred families who acknowledged the new teaching; of these, only fifteen families remained faithful to their teacher. Of the rest many returned to Hinduism; some sold their land, and departed to other places, probably to avoid persecution, or hide their shame.

There were others who outwardly acknowledged the Brahmins, but secretly continued steadfast in their loyalty to the Faqír.

About ten years after this persecution was set on foot, the Faqír was taken very ill. It was evident that he was convinced in his heart that the time of his departure was at hand; for he went back to his own village and home, to prepare for his latter end. He had no son to take his place, so he appointed a nephew to be his successor, and made him take a solemn oath that he would preserve with great care the pamphlet which the Bábá-Jí gave him, and preach his religion everywhere, and look after and take care of his disciples.

When he died, the nephew, in accordance with the oath he had made, put on the garb of a Faqír, and set out to visit his uncle's disciples; but his heart was not in this new religion. He said it was only on account of the oath he remained a Faqír, lest the spirit of his uncle should trouble him.

It was not astonishing to find that he was very careless in the performance of his duties. He did not require from the Satguruwás, like his uncle, any evidence of their faith, nor did he strengthen them in this new religion. He was so careless and indifferent that he did not even forbid them worshipping idols. He was wont to say, 'It is necessary for weak humanity to have some outward symbol of the invisible God through which man can worship Him.' But though the Faqír was lacking in zeal for the new religion, and was far inferior in every respect to his uncle, still the disciples received him with great respect, and gave him the same honour they had accorded to his uncle, and paid him his dues in money and food as they had done to their old teacher.

CHAPTER III.

THE CATECHIST VISITS PHULKIYA.

AT the time when the events recorded in the previous chapter took place, about sixteen miles from Phulkiya, a number of Christians had settled in Sáhibganj. They had obtained work in connection with the railway which passes through that place. The missionary at Bhágalpur sent a catechist, named Hira Lall, to live in their midst, to look after them, and encourage them to show a bright Christian example, and also to preach the Word of God to the heathen around them.

It happened one day, when Babu Hira Lall was preaching in the bazaar to the heathen, he saw three men from the country, apparently cultivators, listening most attentively for a long time to the Word of God. They made signs to one another during the preaching, and it became evident to the catechist that his discourse was most acceptable to them. When he had finished his address, and most of the people were gone away, carrying, it is hoped, some of the precious seed in their hearts, the three men saluted the catechist, and with great eagerness inquired what caste he belonged to; 'for,'

NATIVE CHRISTIANS PREACHING IN A BAZAAR.

said they, 'we also believe in Jesus Christ, and have given up the worship of idols. We are convinced the heathen gods are false.'

On hearing this confession, Babu Hira Lall was very much surprised and perplexed. There was certainly something peculiar and genuine in their confession, so he asked them who they were.

'To outward appearance,' he said, 'you look like Hindus; but how did you become acquainted with the teaching of the Lord Jesus Christ? If you,' continued he, 'ask me what I am, my answer is plain and simple: I am a Christian.'

These cultivators had never heard of Christians, nor did they know that the followers of Jesus were called by that name. They only knew the word 'Christian' as a term of reproach for those who had lost their caste, and had given up their religion. It never occurred to their simple minds that there was any connection between the teaching of Jesus Christ and those persons commonly called Christians. When, therefore, they heard the catechist call himself a Christian, they were astonished, and said, 'What! indeed! Are you a Christian? and do Christians believe in Jesus Christ, and acknowledge our Faqír?'

The catechist and the cultivators had a long talk together, and they told him all about the tract and the Faqír. They continued the conversation till the shades of evening were drawing on, and they were obliged to return to their village. They promised, however, to pay another visit to Sáhibganj in a day or two, and tell the catechist more about their religion, and hear from him more about the doctrines he held. He also ascertained that they lived in Phulkiya.

Babu Hira Lall waited for two or three days, expecting to meet them in the bazaar, but they failed to keep their promise. He therefore started to Phulkiya to find them, and renew the conversation which had taken place in the bazaar. He reached his destination the same evening, tired and worn-out. The people of the village directed him to the house of Dharmdás, who was the appointed minister to teach the Satguruwás the wonders of the little pamphlet. This pamphlet Dharmdás had carefully copied, according to the injunctions of the Faqír, and it was kept with great care.

When Dharmdás saw the catechist he was very pleased, and gave him a hearty welcome. He brought him with great politeness to the inner part of the house, and then fell at his feet and said, 'You have come a long way, and must be very tired, and all this to visit a poor man like me!'

All Indian houses of any pretensions have an inner court or yard, around which the rooms of the house are ranged; and be this ever so small it affords a private place where the people of the house can meet their special friends. Dharmdás thus welcomed the catechist by calling him into the private apartments, and gave him water to wash his hands and feet, according to Eastern custom. He also prepared a place for him in the cow-shed, where he could pass the night; for it opened into the inner court, and afforded a safe resting-place for a visitor.

After the catechist had refreshed himself and rested a little, he and Dharmdás began conversing with great earnestness and affection. When the Babu had heard the story of the Faqír and his disciples more fully, he said, 'Please show the pamphlet which has worked such wonders amongst your people, or read some of it to me;' but Dharmdás replied that he could not, on any consideration, show him the book, as the Bábá-Jí had enjoined them to keep it secret, and not allow any outsider to see it. But this was a mere excuse. He wished to protect it from the unclean touch of Babu Hira Lall, who was a Christian. He was afraid lest, by subjecting it to the touch of a Christian, the Faqír should hear somehow of the conversation, and be angry that he had listened to the teaching of another. Therefore he did not show him the pamphlet.

The catechist then said, 'The gist of the tract has certainly been taken from the Christian Scriptures.' But Dharmdás did not believe him, because the story had become current somehow amongst the disciples of the Faqír, that the pamphlet was found inside a gourd, which fell down from heaven, and was picked up in a field by the Bábá-Jí, who erected his hut outside the village, and whose story has been told in the first chapter. The catechist smiled on hearing this account, and asked Dharmdás whether the original Faqír had originated the story, or his present successor. The question was too much for Dharmdás, and he could not answer. He saw the Babu smile incredulously, but he believed the story all the same, and assured Hira Lall most earnestly that it was indeed true, whether he believed it or not. The Babu thought it wise to say no more about it at present, and told him the story of Jesus Christ from the Gospels. They continued their conversation till midnight.

In the morning all the disciples of the Bábá-Jí came to see the catechist, and listened the whole day to his preaching. They confessed that the true Saviour is indeed the Lord Jesus Christ. The day after, the catechist returned home. There was kindled in his heart a love and affection for these simple-minded people, who with such warmth confessed and worshipped the Lord

Jesus; and there came a longing into his heart to bring them, God helping him, to the full light of the glorious gospel of Jesus Christ.

As soon as Babu Hira Lall reached home, he wrote to the missionary all about the wonderful story he had heard; but, unfortunately, he was unable to pay them a visit at that time. The rainy season was coming on, and the approach to Phulkiya was simply impossible, on account of the country being flooded.

Our readers must understand that Phulkiya is situated on low land in the vicinity of the Ganges. During the rainy season, when the river is in flood, the whole neighbourhood is under water. This necessitates the houses being built on platforms raised about ten feet above the level of the ground. Each household lives on such a raised mound, and thus the streets of the village are about ten or fifteen feet below the level of the houses. The middle of such a raised mound forms a courtyard, and round it the people build their dwelling-places, consisting of four rooms—namely, a room to live in, a cook-room, and two cattle-sheds. In the height of the rains, when the water rises to the level of the courtyards, and often floods them, each household lives, as it were, on a separate island, entirely cut off from their neighbours. The villagers have then to travel by boat to Sâhibganj to buy provisions; and when they visit each other, they swim across, or drive a bullock into the water and hold on by its tail, or they use rafts made of plantain trees. A most ingenious raft, capable of carrying three or four persons, is often made by binding bamboo lattice-work over four earthen vessels, necks downwards.

The missionary wrote to the catechist to say he would come after the rainy season, when it would be possible to approach the village.

CHAPTER IV.

THE MISSIONARY VISITS PHULKIYA, AND SO DOES THE FAQÍR.

ACCORDING to his promise, the missionary visited Phulkiya in the cold season, which follows the rains, and pitched his tent near the village. Then, not only the disciples of the Bábá-Jí, but all the people of the village, gladly came from time to time to hear the Word of God. They all marvelled, and said, 'This is very strange. The Satguruwás say that the religion of Christians and that of the Faqír is alike in many things, but the missionary says the Faqír has taken his doctrines from Christianity, and taught them for his own. Who, indeed, is telling the truth?'

For some time the missionary continued teaching and preaching in Phulkiya, and his daughter told the women the same story of the cross of Christ. The people by degrees began to understand the truths of the Gospel, and the way of salvation through our Lord and Saviour Jesus Christ. In April the missionary was obliged to return to his station. The disciples of the Bábá-Jí were exceedingly sorry when they heard he was going. They besought him not to forget them, for they felt like orphans bereft of their parents, and like children without a teacher. He assured them that, if God spared him, he would visit them again in October. On hearing this they were somewhat comforted, and said, 'Do not forget your promise; as for us, we shall count the days till your return.'

In the following June, the Faqír, their religious teacher, came to Phulkiya. He heard the story of the villagers going to Sáhibganj, and of their conversation with the catechist, and his subsequent visits to them. They also told him about the visit of the missionary, and how wonderfully he had opened the teaching of their little book by referring them to the Gospels. They then took him to the catechist, who told him the wonderful story of the cross as given in the New Testament. The Faqír was filled with astonishment. He remained in the catechist's house for several months, and learned much during this time about the religion of Jesus Christ.

The missionary, hearing that the teacher and Faqír of the Satguruwás had come to Sáhibganj, went to see him; but the Faqír hid himself, and would on no account consent to an interview. When, however, the missionary had returned to Bhágalpur, the Faqír came out of his hiding-place. The catechist asked him why he had run away and disappeared so suddenly. He replied that he was ashamed to meet a minister of the Christian religion; 'for,' said he, 'I am a minister like him, and I was afraid he might ask me many difficult questions, which I should be unable to answer, and do you think that I relish the idea of being made a fool before my disciples? When I am better acquainted with this religion, I will see him.' He then begged to be allowed to take his leave of Babu Hira Lall, and proceed on his itinerations amongst the Satguruwás. The catechist did his best to persuade him to remain longer; but the Faqír persisted in his purpose, and, having purchased a New Testament and several tracts, he proceeded on his journey. He did not, however, forbid his disciples mixing and holding converse with the Christians, and so they began to be even more friendly than ever.

Whenever the catechist visited Phulkiya, the Satguruwás were delighted to see him. He was welcomed as a guest in their houses, and waited upon with the greatest attention. All idea of remuneration for their hospitality they rejected as absurd, and each was anxious to do him some little service. When he reproved them for being over-solicitous about his wants, they replied, 'You are our teacher, and take all this trouble to come and instruct us; surely you will allow us to repay you as far as we can for your kindness?'

The Satguruwás were always delighted to hear the Word of God. When the catechist used to go and preach to them, they left their work willingly, and sat beside him, and for hours, yea, sometimes till the middle of the night, they would remain engaged in conversation on this important topic. But when he ventured to suggest to them that they should be baptized, and take upon themselves the open profession of Christianity, they became indifferent, and said, 'We cannot consent to give up our caste. Do we not believe in Jesus Christ? Do we call upon any other name but the name of the Lord? Have we hope in any other? Why should we therefore give up our caste? No, Babu; we cannot on any account do what you advise.'

In the cold season, when the missionary came again to visit them, it was evident that the Satguruwás had made great progress in the knowledge and faith of our

Lord and Saviour, but they had not the least intention of becoming Christians. The catechist, Hira Lall, began to grow impatient; but the missionary advised him not to hasten such matters by the spirit of impatience, as it is impossible to force people to become Christians. 'It will be better,' said he, 'to go on teaching them, and when the Lord Jesus sees fit He will open their eyes by the Holy Spirit of God, and they will themselves seek baptism, and come into the fold of Christ. Till then, brother, be instant in season and out of season; watch and pray.'

CHAPTER V.

THE WIDOW BHAKTIN.

AMONG the Satguruwás of Phulkiya there was a poor widow, who earned her daily bread by working as a labourer in the fields. When, during the rains, the work in the fields was practically stopped, would carry bundles of grain and rice on her head for the cultivators to the market at Sáhibganj, and thus earn an honest living. The people called her *Bhaktin*, 'the pious one,' and this was a very appropriate name, for indeed she was very good and religious. This poor widow had passed through much trial and sorrow. Her husband died soon after they were married, and from that time she was obliged to earn her daily bread and provide for her daughter. This daughter was very good-looking, and she ultimately married into a very respectable family. After the marriage had taken place, the mother was comforted with the thought that she would always be able, in the case of need, to find a home with her daughter, and thus pass her days in peace.

According to the custom of the country, the marriage took place when the girl was a mere child; but when the girl grew up to woman's estate she was conducted with the usual ceremony to the house of her husband. Strange to say, soon after her arrival, she suddenly disappeared in a mysterious manner. She was sought for everywhere, but not a trace of her could be found; and nobody knew what had become of her. Some said that possibly, when she went to the river to fetch water, or to bathe, an alligator must have devoured her; others, that she must have gone into the jungle close by the village, and been seized by a tiger or a bear. Again, others thought that she had been led astray by bad people, and conveyed by them to other parts of the country. Some said one thing, some said another; but the mystery of her sudden disappearance still remained, and no one could throw any light on the question. The poor mother in consequence was nearly beside herself. Sometimes she would cry aloud, in her grief, 'Would to God my child had been burnt[1] before my eyes, then I should have been comforted! Where can I find comfort, and who will bring me news of my lost one?'

Just about the time this trial came to Bhaktin, the Faqír appeared at Phulkiya, and Bhaktin told him all her sorrow, and became one of his disciples. The Faqír advised her to give up idolatry, and believe on the Lord Jesus Christ, the true Incarnation, and pray to Him in her trouble. He found Bhaktin a very pliable pupil and a devoted disciple, doing and observing all he commanded her. When, however, the catechist came to Phulkiya, and preached the way of the Lord more fully, she became one of his most zealous followers. As she gradually received instruction, her improvement in religion and piety was manifest to all who knew her. The people living near used to say she was the best woman they ever knew.

[1] On the funeral pile.

Although Bhaktin was only a daily labourer, and had to earn her bread by the sweat of her brow, still she was ever ready to help the needy as far as possible. When any one was taken ill, she would go, uncalled for, to minister to them in their sickness, asking and seeking no remuneration. When she saw any one in great sorrow, she would do her best to administer comfort and consolation. Gradually she became such a general favourite that every one told her their sorrow and trouble, and asked her advice in difficulties.

Bhaktin's disposition was that of a little child, simple and trustful. Whatever she heard that was worthy of belief, and useful in religious life, she accepted at once, and carried out into practice. Before she knew the Christians, and was only acting on the teaching of the Faqír, she had a firm belief in the mercy of God and the power of prayer. On several occasions she had prayed so earnestly for sick people that many of them had been raised up again, evidently in answer to her prayers. When she became acquainted with the missionary and his daughter, one day, as the latter was giving a lesson on the nature and power of prayer, Bhaktin said, with great warmth, 'It is true, it is true the Lord hears prayer; but I have been puzzled to know how it was that when Madho's son was very ill last year, I had to pray all night for his recovery before God heard our prayer; for it was only in the morning we observed signs of returning strength. His parents were bigoted Hindus, but when the boy got better the mother said, "Your Christ is great and powerful, and I shall begin to pray to Him." The husband, however, was an enemy of the Satguruwás, and, having heard his wife's profession of faith, beat her severely, and told her to take care not to mention the name of Jesus in his house. He spoke angrily to me also,' said Bhaktin, 'and used abusive language, and turned me out of the house. But what can he do? Can he beat his wife's faith out of her? It is impossible. Outwardly his wife continues to worship idols, but in her heart she believes in Jesus, the true Incarnation. It is quite possible,' continued Bhaktin, 'that the Lord did not answer my prayer all at once, because her husband was a hard-hearted, bigoted man; but, you see, God did hear my prayer at last, and raised up the boy.'

There was no anger or enmity in the heart of Bhaktin. People might laugh at her and make fun of her, but she always bore it in the spirit of meekness, and with great patience. To her own people she would say, 'Let them laugh; they are blind, and know not what they do. When their eyes are opened they will know better.'

Another day, the missionary's daughter was teaching the wives of the disciples of the Faqír, and encouraging them to remain firm in the faith, and not be moved by fear or persecution. Bhaktin feelingly said, 'For ten years, since I became a disciple of the Faqír, I have endured many trials and temptations, and shall I give up my faith now because of a few difficulties? Never, never! It is impossible!'

Bhaktin had a niece called Tulsiya, whose husband's name was Lálá. They lived about a day and a half's journey from Phulkiya. Tulsiya came now and then to see her parents, and her aunt used to give her lessons on these occasions in the religion of the Bábá-Jí, which was all she knew in those days. When Tulsiya was thirteen years of age, she first became aware of the fact that it is a sin to worship idols, and that the Bábá-Jí's religion was founded on truth. From that time she began to pray to Jesus Christ. At first her father-in-law, thinking she would soon forget it, told his family to let her alone and say nothing. 'She has been taught these strange notions by her aunt,' said he; 'and when the Hindu festival comes round she will join in the festivities like the rest of us.'

But Tulsiya remained firm to her convictions. Slowly and surely it occurred to her that if the worship of idols was a sin, then all offerings that were made, and sweetmeats that were given and eaten in their name, were sinful also, and that therefore she could not join in the festivals, nor adorn herself for these occasions. When she refused to join in the heathen festivities, and went and sat apart alone, her father-in-law and all his people were very much distressed. They asked her, in a loving, gentle way, why she was acting thus. 'Rejoice with us,' they said; but Tulsiya would not, and then her relatives began to be angry with her. Tulsiya begged to be allowed to go and see her father and mother; but they refused, on the plea that she would be confirmed in her new opinions by the influence of her aunt. Thus Tulsiya did not see her people for more than a year and a half. She was not aware that in the meantime the Gospel of Jesus had been preached in Phulkiya by the missionary and catechist.

CHAPTER VI.

THE CLOUDS BEGIN TO GATHER.

NEXT cold season found the missionary again in Phulkiya. The disciples of the Bábá-Jí requested him to conduct divine service in their village, and not in the tent as usual. They urged that the people in the village wished to attend a Christian service, and there would not be room for all in his tent; they wanted to prepare a room in the village for this purpose. The missionary was exceedingly pleased to conduct service wherever they wished. He felt it was decidedly a gain to be allowed to carry the Gospel into their very houses; for although his tent was on the outskirts of the village, some of those who were shy would not venture to go to a missionary's tent to hear the Gospel.

On receiving permission from the missionary, Dharmdás, who had a very roomy cow-shed, ordered it to be cleaned thoroughly. He spread matting on the floor, and put a curtain at one end of it, to screen off the women from the men; and from that time divine service was conducted in the village. When the people heard the harmonium they were very much astonished, never having heard such an instrument before. Besides, the native Christian hymns which were sung were accompanied by various native musical instruments, which, though strange to a European ear, have a peculiar charm to the native mind. And so *bhajans* and native Christian hymns were sung, and one and all, Satguruwás and Hindus, joined with heart and soul in the singing. It was an interesting sight to see them all gathered together, joining, however ignorantly and imperfectly, in a Christian service. For some time after this the people of the village did not trouble the Satguruwás about their religion. All was peace and harmony.

The proverb, however, is true all over the world, 'Satan finds some mischief still for idle hands to do.' The spirit of opposition after a time began again to manifest itself. One day Dharmdás and Premdás came to the tent, and wished to see the missionary. Premdás had not been a Satguruwá long, but Dharmdás and he were old friends. When Dharmdás heard the catechist preach in the bazaar on that memorable occasion, Premdás was also one of the hearers. The Word of God made a great impression on his heart, and from that time he had accepted the religion of the Satguruwás. The Spirit of the Lord had influenced him so far that he was now more zealous and sincere than Dharmdás, the village leader of the Satguruwás.

Dharmdás and Premdás opened the conversation by saying, 'We are sorry to inform you that the people of the village accuse us of being Christians. Will you kindly tell them that we are not Christians, and do not intend to become Christians? We only worship the Lord Jesus, and receive Him into our hearts, because our teacher and Faqír said He is the true Incarnation and Saviour of the Satguruwás. We have not given up caste, and never will. The people, however, do not believe what we say; but if you will take our side, they will be mollified.'

The missionary, with much gentleness, replied, 'I am convinced, brethren, you are not far from the kingdom of God, and will soon become servants of the Lord Jesus, and be baptized. You are now standing between heaven and earth—will you always remain in this spirit of indecision? You have, as it were, got one foot in one boat and the other in another. Go on in this good way: decide to cross the river in one boat only, the boat belonging to Jesus Christ, and then you will gain your end, and be saved.'

The missionary added further words of exhortation, and begged them to make their choice now, wisely and prayerfully. But somehow they did not elect to take his advice. They went away much troubled, yea, almost despondent, and said to one another, 'What shall we do? This is a great difficulty. How shall we extricate ourselves from it?' The idea of giving up caste seemed impossible to them; for they reasoned after a human fashion, and said, 'If so much persecution is our lot as Satguruwás, how much greater will it be if we give up our caste and become Christians! We should not be allowed to draw water from the well, the oilman would not sell us oil, the grocer would not allow us to enter his shop to buy food, the barber would refuse to shave us, the washerman would not wash our clothes, the cow-herd would object to graze our cattle,—and then how would it be possible for us to live? We should quickly perish. Besides, no one would give their sons and daughters to our children in marriage; everything would be against us.' Such thoughts found expression as they reasoned together; they were sincerely troubled and alarmed, and at last became utterly despondent.

The catechist, Hira Lall, tried in vain to administer comfort. He showed them their plain duty, and told them how many Hindus had become Christians, and how they managed to exist in comparative comfort. God would protect them, if only they would make a venture of faith, and come over to the Lord's side. No real impression, however, was made on their hearts, and from that time these two men tried to avoid the missionary, and almost ceased to converse with him whenever he crossed their path.

This was the state of things when the hot season set in. The missionary was obliged to return to Bhágalpur on account of the heat, but before going away he went to every house, and gave each family a word of advice, and having prayed with them, he left them to the working of the God of providence who doeth all things well. When the tents were struck, and all was ready for the journey, the Satguruwás advised the catechist also to return to Sáhibganj, as the people had now become suspicious of his presence too. What could Babu Hira Lall do? He could not force the people to allow him to stay, for they were free agents. He therefore arranged to return home. Before starting, however, he reasoned with and begged them most earnestly not to forget what they had been taught. As the result of this earnest pleading, they consented to his coming over every Sunday to conduct divine service for them.

When the Hindus of the village saw the result of the pressure they had brought to bear on the Satguruwás, and how fickle and double-minded they had become, they began to persecute them more than ever. This was done to induce them not to associate with Christians; and although there was no hope of their ever becoming Hindus again, still they expected it would hinder them from becoming Christians. With this object in view, they caused their crops to be eaten up, enticed away their servants, and refused to buy from them or sell to them. Thus all the evils they predicted would follow on their becoming Christians even now fell on their heads.

In every village there is what is called a *Puncháyat*, or village committee, to settle all religious and social disputes. This committee exercises unbounded sway over the social customs of the people. It fines, punishes, and excommunicates all miscreants, and woe to the man who attempts to set aside its decision! In their difficulty the disciples of the Bábá-Jí appealed to the village Puncháyat, and asked why they were thus being persecuted. Did they think them Christians?

The chairman of the Puncháyat said in reply, 'If you are not Christians, why do you receive in your midst a Christian teacher and worship with him? If you will cease to attend his meetings, and refuse to listen to the missionary when he comes, we shall have nothing to say against you. You can still continue to acknowledge your Faqír, and remain Satguruwás.' They were again reproved and frightened, and informed that if they did not consent to do as advised, such and such things would happen to them.

In this way the disciples of the Bábá-Jí were awed by the village assembly, and in fear they said one to another, 'Brothers, we are helpless; we cannot withstand such opposition; we shall perish if we persist.' Even Dharmdás, who was the leader of the Satguruwás in the village, began to quail in the presence of such opposition. Having heard the threats and reproaches of the Puncháyat, he was led astray, and was prepared to consent to the demands of those who opposed the Gospel. But Premdás

took a firm stand, and said, 'If all of you desert this good cause and the missionary, I for one will remain faithful to him and the catechist. This religion is true, and I will not give it up. If Brother Dharmdás refuses to receive the catechist when he comes, then I will find a place for him in my house.'

When the members of the Puncháyat heard this bold and decided declaration from Premdás, a great tumult arose in their midst; some said one thing, and some another. Friends and enemies attacked Premdás most unmercifully, and said, 'Who are you, to talk in this fashion? Are you able to oppose yourself to the decision of this Puncháyat, and can you cope with us?' Several of his enemies chuckled, and said, 'Very well; we shall see who is the strongest, and how long this perverseness will continue. You will see what further troubles will come upon you.' They then dismissed the assembly, as nothing could be done.

CHAPTER VII.

THE STORM BREAKS.

EIGHT days after the Puncháyat, the grass roof of Premdás' house was all in flames. The poor helpless creatures were unable to save any of their property, because the stream and the well were far away, and there was no one to give a helping hand. The flames spread rapidly to all the four rooms of the house. His two dwelling-rooms, cook-house, and cow-shed were soon burnt to the ground; nothing but the mud walls remained. Their clothes, furniture, and grain were consumed in the flames. Only the cows and animals which fled from the house were saved. In a short space of time all was over, and Premdás had time to ponder over what had happened. No one knew how the building took fire; but Premdás and his friends remembered the threats of one or two in the Puncháyat: 'We shall see,' they said; 'something will befall you.' Premdás' suspicions were aroused; he felt sure an enemy had done it. Great difficulties faced him as the result of this calamity. The rainy season was nearly over, but there was no dry grass as yet to be had for thatching; his house had to remain roofless; still he said, 'Let them do what they like, I will not give up my religion.'

But there were other troubles looming in the distance. Premdás felt he could overcome this calamity in time, but other difficulties faced him. The face of Dharmdás had not been the same to him during the past few weeks as in days gone by; a cloud gathered on his brow when he met Premdás. When Dharmdás saw that Premdás had determined to receive the catechist if he refused, he changed his mind, and said he would continue to receive him as usual, but showed by his manner that the visits were most unwelcome to him. Babu Hira Lall was a shrewd man, and quickly perceived that the mind of Dharmdás was hostile to the Gospel. He heard also that Premdás only stood firm and faithful in the Punchávat. This led him naturally to prefer the society of Premdás, who had shown such a spirit of loyalty to the Lord Jesus. He tried to strengthen and comfort him; and when this calamity overtook him, Hira Lall began to love him more and more, and he could not help showing it. His frequent visits to Premdás' house caused a feeling of jealousy to spring up in the mind of Dharmdás, and Premdás observed that his old friend Dharmdás did not feel at ease in his presence; he even avoided him. Can we wonder that Premdás was troubled, and that sorrow filled his heart?

When the villagers saw that their threats and persecutions had no effect on Premdás, they left him in peace, and began to turn the fury of their persecution on another Satguruwá. This man was a leper, named Jethú. He had only a finger and a thumb on his right hand, and was so helpless that he was unable to feed himself. When the missionary came first to Phulkiya, his daughter taught Jethú to eat with a spoon, which he held by his finger and thumb. This was a great comfort to him, and he would often in his joy say, 'What a blessing that I am now able to feed myself!'

Jethú's wife would have nothing to do with the Christians; she persecuted her husband a great deal about religion, and asked him continually what was the good of all these new ideas? why did he not walk in the same old way in which his fathers had trod? Several times she threatened to run away, and did actually run from his house, saying, 'Until you do as I wish, I shall not return to your house, so you may manage as best you can.' Although Jethú suffered much from her flights of temper and disobedience, still he never gave way to the wishes of his wife. As a rule, when her anger cooled down, she would return to him, and minister to his wants and necessities. The people of the village took his wife's part, and threatened that, if he refused to listen to their requests, and opposed them, some calamity would surely befall his eldest son. The boy, who was fourteen years of age, was the staff and comfort of his afflicted father, and did all his work. After some days the lad was found drowned in a tank near the village. It was not known how it had taken place.

This was a great calamity and sorrow to the father, and his wife added to his affliction by accusing him of being the cause of it. 'It is all your fault,' she said; 'my promising, fine-looking boy is lost to us through your perversity and obtuseness; and who knows what will befall us next?' But the more Jethú tried to comfort his wife in this sorrow, the more she poured her maledictions upon him and persecuted him.

The disciples of the Bábá-Jí were filled with fear and apprehension for the future. They did not know what would be the end of all their troubles; for, behold,

Premdás' house had been burnt to the ground, and Jethú's son drowned, and who knew what would follow? They therefore sent a message to the missionary, through the catechist, begging him to discontinue his visits, lest some worse calamity should befall the community.

The missionary consented to their request; and, when camping season came again, he pitched his tent about four miles from Phulkiya, and preached to the people in those villages. He knew very well that the disciples of the Bábá-Jí were sure to seek him out; and so it happened. They would come secretly at night, and tell him all their sorrows and troubles, hear the Word of God and join in prayer; but still they had no intention of becoming Christians. When the missionary pleaded with them, and enjoined them to receive Christ, they always gave their old excuse—that if there was so much persecution now, how much more there would be on their becoming Christians, and how could they manage to live? It was better for them to remain disciples of the Bábá-Jí, and in their hearts be faithful to the Lord Jesus.

About this time it became known to the missionary, that the pamphlet which Dharmdás had copied by order of the Faqír, and which he had preserved so carefully from the vulgar eye, not allowing even a Christian to see it, was the work of a German missionary, Mr. Sternberg. The pamphlet was called *Gyándípak*, ' The Lamp of Wisdom,' and was printed at the Mission Press, Muzaffarpur. The missionary was exceedingly glad to obtain this information, for he saw now the way to convince the Satguruwás that the Bábá-Jí had taken his religion from Christianity, and that the story about it having been sent direct from heaven to the Bábá-Jí was a falsehood. The missionary sent for one hundred copies of it, in order to distribute them amongst the Satguruwás and others.

CHAPTER VIII.

THE PAMPHLET AND ITS STORY.

NE night, when the disciples of the Bábá-Jí came again to see the missionary, he showed them the copies of the *Gyándípak*, 'The Lamp of Wisdom.' Dharmdás asked what books they were. The missionary requested him to take one and read it. He took up a copy, and began to read it. All at once he turned towards his brethren with a troubled look, and said, with some concern, 'Why, this is all like our Bábá-Jí's book!'

Each of them took a copy of the book, and began to turn it over in their hands; for none of them save Dharmdás could read. In the meantime, Dharmdás, in a trembling voice, but with spirit and evident interest, read on. After a short time he turned to the missionary in surprise and confusion, and said excitedly, 'Why, this is the very thing! this is *our* book! How did you get it?' The missionary smiled, and assured Dharmdás that it was not *their* pamphlet, but one issued from a Mission Press some years before their religion was known; that it was written by a missionary; and that all the information and instruction in it had been taken from the Word of God. 'Your original Bábá-Jí,' he said, 'must have obtained a copy from some missionary or catechist.'

The missionary thought all their belief in this new religion would melt away on hearing the truth and the real history of the pamphlet; but, on the contrary, they clung with tenacity to the Bábá-Jí's religion, and only hung down their heads and looked troubled. Before their eyes the foundations of the Satguruwás' religion were being undermined, and the building was tottering to its fall, and they knew now that Christianity was the true source of all their teaching. Few men could give up their religion without a struggle, even though it may be a false one; we can really sympathise with these men. There was no spirit left in them, and none of them could utter a word. Becoming thoroughly dejected, they began to look at one another, and walked silently in the darkness outside; but, at the request of the missionary, each took a copy of the *Gyándípak* with him.

During the year of which we are writing, the production of the original pamphlet produced no visible result. The fear of the Satguruwás did not abate, and their faith made no apparent progress. They avoided the missionary more than ever, and only came to see him once after this remarkable interview, when they heard he was returning to his station. Seeing the turn things were taking, Babu Hira Lall, the catechist, lost all hope, and said to the missionary, 'I cannot now go each Sunday to Phulkiya to conduct divine service, because it will do no good. Besides, Dharmdás does not receive me now with the same brotherly feeling as in the past. He is angry with me for some reason, and I have tried to explain to him that I have no desire to trouble him any more, and would stay with Premdás, but he would not consent to my arrangement. I think it will be better for me to discontinue my visits to Phulkiya for a time.'

The missionary, after a few words of encouragement, advised the catechist not to discontinue his visits so long as the Satguruwás were willing to receive him. Until they themselves positively refused to listen to him, it would not be right in the sight of God to leave them without witness. 'I am sure,' he said, 'the Lord Jesus will not now forsake them. Will He allow those who have come so far out of darkness towards the light to perish? He will bring them, I am sure, to the full light of the Gospel. Let us trust God in this matter, dear brother, and do our duty with patience, "for in due season we shall reap if we faint not."'

When the missionary reached Bhágalpur, he called the Christians together, and, as was his custom at such times, recounted all that the Lord had done during this camping season. The congregation had heard on previous occasions all about the interesting work going on amongst the Satguruwás, and they had assured one another that this year some would come forth and declare themselves on the Lord's side. But when they heard that, instead of advancing in the faith, they were evidently going back, they were much disappointed and troubled. They arranged amongst themselves to meet once a week to pray for them, and ask the Lord of the harvest to have mercy on their infirmity, and revive their faith, which, like a flickering candle, appeared to be going out, and to give them courage to come out from amongst their people, and take upon them the yoke of Christ.

The Christians therefore met together once a week to pray for the disciples of the Bábá-Jí. The missionary also bore them upon his heart in private and family devotions. God does indeed hear the prayers of His servants, and their request finds a willing listener in Him. This was singularly made manifest to all the brethren in Bhágalpur who were praying for the Satguruwás.

Although it appeared as if the work of the Lord was going back in Phulkiya, in reality it was not so. Premdás and Bhaktin remained firm in the faith, but from a feeling of fear did not say much about it. Tulsiya, too, was walking in the truth as far as she had light and knowledge. It will be remembered that on account of the objections of the Satguruwás, the missionary had pitched his tent that year in Mahaganj, and not in Phulkiya. Whilst he was there, Tulsiya obtained permission from her father-in-law to visit her home for a month. As soon as she reached her father's house, she heard the missionary had often visited the village. On one occasion she had an interview with the catechist. She also heard of the trials and sufferings of the Satguruwás, and how much they had endured for their religion since the missionary and catechist had come amongst them. When the missionary visited Phulkiya that year, Tulsiya would watch him enter the village, but never ventured to speak to him. None of the disciples of the Bábá-Jí told him Tulsiya's story, and inasmuch as the missionary's daughter did not accompany her father this year, neither he nor his daughter knew the story of the girl's trials and sorrows. Tulsiya's father was wavering in his adherence to the religion of the Bábá-Jí, and he began to associate with the Satguruwás less and less, and was ready to return to the worship of idols. Sometimes he complained that ever since the missionary and the catechist began to visit them, all sorts of trials had come upon them. But this was not really true, for before they knew them the Satguruwás had to suffer for their religion. He continually rebuked his sister Bhaktin, and told her to give up all this nonsense, or he would turn her out of his house. He also became very angry with his daughter Tulsiya for clinging to the Christians' God. When a month had passed away, Tulsiya's father-in-law came to fetch her; but she pleaded and expostulated, saying, 'I will not go so soon; I have come home after so long a time, and I must remain longer.' But her father-in-law refused to allow her to remain any longer. Tulsiya fell at his and her father's feet, and with great earnestness besought them to allow her to remain a little longer. At last her father relented, and said to her father-in-law, ' Let her stay on; I will take this nonsense out of her head.'

Her father-in-law, being helpless in the matter, was obliged to return home alone. Her father was indeed very anxious that all the members of his family should not only give up the idea of becoming Christians, but also that they should give up the Bábá-Jí's religion, and walk in the footsteps of their forefathers. Every day he was persecuting his daughter and sister on account of their strong religious impressions, which he said were favourable to Christianity; and when neither of them would agree to his suggestions he was furious with them, and went so far as to beat his daughter on several occasions. Tulsiya, however, was not convinced, and whenever she found herself alone with her aunt, she always talked about religion and truth. She listened to her aunt's simple words of faith, and was much comforted and strengthened. When her father-in-law came again to take her home, she was much stronger in the faith than when she came, and her father knew this, though he professed to ignore it. He rebuked her fiercely when giving her over to her father-in-law, and said to the latter, 'Take her away, and do not bring her here again; she has become more and more obstinate.' Poor Tulsiya wept much and sorrowfully as she followed her father-in-law home.

CHAPTER IX.

A STEP ONWARDS.

IN the beginning of the rains, Babu Hira Lall went on Saturday as usual to conduct divine service on the following day. Dharmdás received him with great respect and apparent affection, as he was wont to do in the past, before all the disturbance occurred. When the two entered into conversation that evening, the reason for this change in his conduct soon became apparent. Dharmdás told the Babu he had felt a wish for some time to visit Bhágalpur, and see the missionary and congregation of Christians, in order to ascertain their manner of life, and how they managed to get a living. 'Will you go with me?' said he; 'for I cannot go alone.'

It must be confessed that during the time the Satguruwás had exhibited such strange conduct, even after they knew the real truth about the book, Babu Hira Lall had become very sceptical about their conversion to Christianity, and he had almost ceased to believe there was any good in them. He was delighted, as may be imagined, with this request, though it rebuked his unbelief, and he replied with warmth of feeling, 'Your desire to visit Bhágalpur is praiseworthy and good, but if you will kindly take one or two others with you, it will be better. Premdás will be willing to accompany us, I am sure.'

Dharmdás objected, and wished to know why Premdás should go with them; he said he preferred to take some one else instead. This offered a fair opportunity for the catechist to speak to him of his past conduct to Premdás. He showed him how wrong it was to treat an old friend in this way. At last he persuaded him to have an understanding somehow with his old friend.

The catechist and Dharmdás went that very night to Premdás' house. The latter was astonished, as might be expected, to see them; but he received them with every sign of love and friendship. Through the Babu's influence, these two old friends were reconciled. Premdás was delighted with the idea of going to Bhágalpur, and said, 'This has been my heart's desire for some time, and God has shown me how that desire will be gratified.'

On Monday morning, these three, along with another Satguruwá, set out for Bhágalpur. The Christian congregation were delighted and surprised to see them, and so was the missionary. They knew now that their prayers had been heard, and that God was drawing the Satguruwás to Himself. They received them with much affection, and for a couple of weeks entertained them in their houses, and each evening they met for prayer and the singing of Christian hymns. They showed them the Christian village, and told them how happy they all were. They took them also to see the Mission school and church, and, in fact, showed them everything.

These simple villagers had never before seen any large well-built house or building. On seeing the church, they were astonished at its size and durability. It seemed to reach to the sky compared with their grass huts. Out of mere covetousness, they said, 'If such a church were built in Phulkiya, all would soon become Christians.'

Babu Hira Lall smiled, and said, 'My dear friends, the soil of your village is all sand; it would be impossible to make bricks of it, and therefore impossible to erect such a building. Christianity is not such a light thing as that. No one can become a Christian till his spiritual eyes are opened by the Holy Spirit of God, and till his heart is turned by the Lord Jesus Christ.' The Satguruwás sighed, and said, 'Surely you speak the truth. May the Lord look upon us in mercy!'

The Satguruwás were astonished by all they saw and heard. When they saw the arrangements in the Mission for teaching the children, training the orphans, and protecting widows, the Mission servants, teachers, and preachers, and when they became aware of the fact that all these were either under the protection of or in the service of the Mission, then the idea struck them that if they became Christians they and their wives and children also would be provided for, and there would be no fear for the future. They ventured to hint their surmises on this question to Babu Hira Lall.

It was indeed foolish for them to get such an idea in their heads, but we are recording facts of experience, and it is well that men should know the first difficulty that faces the missionary. Eastern human nature is very strange in its workings, and it is perhaps difficult for Europeans to see matters in their way of looking at things. One would expect the catechist to be the first man to disabuse them of such an idea. It was not so in this case, and is not so in many others. The Babu was human, and weak in the faith. He saw the

Satguruwás were inclined to become Christians, and he knew that if the fear of future poverty could be removed from their minds they possibly would make a venture of faith. He saw in this idea of *protection* a human way of getting out of the difficulty. He certainly did not say that their widows and children and poor would be provided for, but he and the other Christians implied that when they became Christians a Mission would be started among them, and a school set on foot, and a European missionary live amongst them. The Babu did not explain to the Satguruwás that it was necessary, in order to carry on a Mission, to have servants, teachers, and preachers, but that it did not necessarily follow that converts would be provided for. He did not show them how wrong it is for men on becoming Christians to expect the Mission to support them. No; he was anxious to institute a motive to remove their difficulties, and he thought this motive would serve his purpose.

It soon became evident, on mixing with the Christians, that the worldly and spiritual eyes of the Satguruwás were being opened, and they kept on saying, 'We are blind; we are very ignorant, and know nothing; we have been growing up like a herd of buffaloes.' When the Christians saw the simplicity and ingenuousness of these men, a feeling of interest sprang up in their hearts, and they began to show them much Christian love. And the poor Satguruwás, who had always been looked upon as enemies by their heathen neighbours, when they saw and experienced the brotherly affection of the Christians, longed to enter into fellowship and cast in their lot with them. In their excitement and happiness, they went to the missionary, and said, 'Christianity is the true and best religion; whatever takes place, we have determined to become Christians. Please baptize us at once.'

But the missionary did not deem it advisable to be in a hurry in such a weighty matter as this. He had his doubts that if they became Christians at this juncture, they would hide the fact from the people of their village; and he knew that, if they did declare it, their wives would certainly run away from them. He therefore advised them to return home and be baptized, together with their families, in Phulkiya, the coming cold season, before all the people of the village. But they were not pleased with this decision; for they were afraid that, if they were baptized before the people of the village, they would kill them. The missionary wisely refused to alter his decision, and said, 'I do not deem it advisable to do a thing like this in a hurry. You have seen the love and friendship which exists amongst the Christians, and you long to partake of it, but perhaps, if you were baptized now, and went to your homes, your love by and by would cool down, and you would be sorry for having acted in such haste; perhaps you would say the Christians had used undue influence to persuade you to join them. Therefore I think you should return as you are to your village, and if in deed and in truth you desire to become Christians, then an opportunity will be afforded you afterwards of doing so.'

The Satguruwás went away very much disappointed, and returned to Phulkiya. But after a month they came back to Bhágalpur, and besought the missionary to receive them into the Christian Church at once, and afterwards to baptize their wives and children in the village. They also informed the missionary that none of the other Satguruwás save Jethú wished to become Christians. Some had certainly said, they added, 'You become Christians first, and when we see how it works, then we shall gain confidence, and perhaps join you.' Thus the three men entreated the missionary to baptize them. 'Whatever is required of us,' they said, 'in the baptismal service, we have learned by heart. The catechist has taught us everything, and we are ready. With heart and soul we desire to become the servants of the Lord Jesus Christ, for He is our only Lord and Saviour.'

After the Satguruwás had spoken so plainly, and declared their faith in the Lord Jesus in such simple terms, the missionary felt it would be wrong to withhold baptism any longer, so he promised to perform the ceremony on the following Lord's day. This Sunday was a high day in the Mission, and one of great joy to the missionary and catechists of Bhágalpur. They had prayed for this day from on high, and it had come, an earnest of future blessing. The three inquirers, however, were much exercised in mind; they were troubled and fearful, wondering what the people of Phulkiya would do when they heard they had become Christians. But the Lord gave them courage and strength to come forth boldly before the congregation and declare their faith. They were received into Christ's flock, and the prayer was offered 'that hereafter they would not be ashamed to confess the faith of Christ crucified, and fight under His banner against the world, the flesh, and the devil.' On Monday, after much prayer and many blessings, they set out for their village.

When the Hindus of Phulkiya heard what had taken place, there were no bounds to their anger, and in great fury they came, and swore before the new converts that they would destroy both them and their families. They so frightened and threatened the wives of these three men, and all the women, yea, even the wives of the Satguruwás, that all of them fled except Bhaktin. They sent their husbands word that they would not return, as they had lost their caste. During the whole of the rains the people of the village boycotted the Satguruwás, and especially the three Christians; and when the floods came and surrounded their houses as usual, no one came to see them, and they visited nobody. Besides this, the catechist could not visit them either, on account of the flood, and these three Christians and all the Satguruwás were without spiritual help or comfort.

CHAPTER X.

BHAKTIN TURNED ADRIFT BY HER BROTHER.

AMONG the disciples of the Bábá-Jí, Jethú Mandal was the most afflicted, especially on account of his wife having run away to her father's house when the three Satguruwás came back to Phulkiya as baptized Christians. The Satguruwás and Bhaktin helped him as much as possible; still he was very helpless. Sometimes, when he was perfectly alone in the house at night, he positively wept aloud, and all the neighbours could hear him crying in distraction of mind and body. Possibly his wife heard about his extreme distress and pain, or maybe the Lord put it into her heart to return to her poor suffering husband; she relented, anyhow, and returned to him at the end of August, and began to minister to his wants as before. But she was not in a right frame of mind; the whole day she was continually quarrelling with him, and went about her work grumbling at everything. The fact is, she wished him to give up his religion, and this was her way of showing her ill-feeling at his apparent obstinacy. Although Jethú was comforted by her kindly help and ministrations, yet he had much to suffer and to endure.

In this way things went on till the end of September. The rains began to abate, and the floods decreased; the fields gradually became visible above the waters. Then all the Satguruwás went to seek their wives, who had run away during the scare about the three men becoming Christians, and God in His mercy inclined their hearts towards their husbands, and they were persuaded to return home. Babu Hira Lall also began to visit them again, to conduct divine service. The catechist was getting old and stiff, and was obliged henceforth to travel in a native cart. He conducted the service in Dharmdás' cow-shed as at first, and things settled down to the same state as they were before the three Satguruwás were baptized.

After a time it became evident that Bhaktin's brother had altogether separated himself from the Satguruwás; he neither attended service nor fraternised with them. He affirmed that he had paid a fine to the Brahmins, and expected to be received back into Hinduism. He was very angry with his sister Bhaktin, because she still held converse with the three Christians and with Babu Hira Lall, and always attended divine service. His reproofs and scoldings were of no avail, for she refused to obey him in this matter. She wished to become a Christian, and had decided in her own mind that, when the wives and children of the three Christians were baptized in the cold season, she would also ask to be received into the Christian Church. But she was very much afraid of her brother, and kept her desire a profound secret.

On Sunday, when the hour for service arrived, Bhaktin, according to custom, prepared to proceed to Dharmdás' house. On seeing her prepare to go, her brother became furious, and glared at her like a tiger in his rage, and said, 'You shall not go there any more; sit down where you are.'

Bhaktin besought her brother not to get angry, as she was perfectly willing to obey him in everything save this matter. She would only go to the service, and return at once. On hearing her determined refusal to obey him

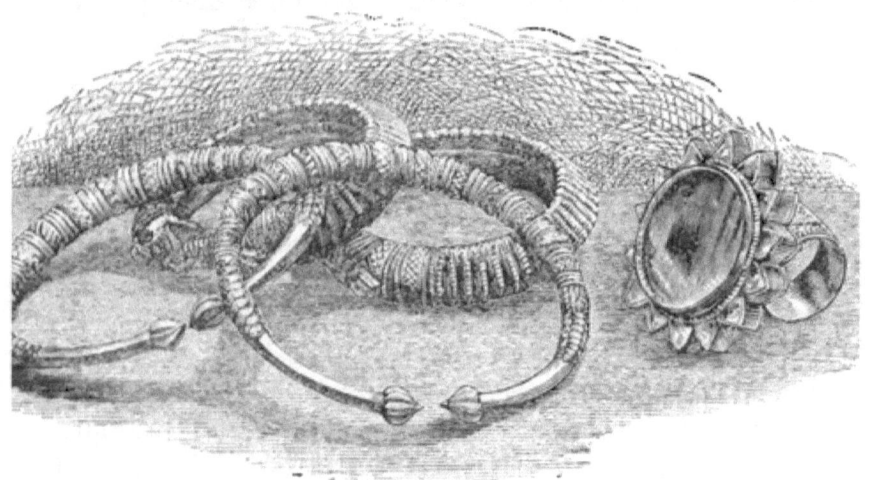

WOMEN'S JEWELS.

in this one thing, he became more furious, and stormed and said, 'If you go there, you will remain; for you shall not show your face in this house again.'

Bhaktin replied, 'Forgive me, dear brother; I cannot neglect the service of God. I have no wish to disobey you, but I must attend worship.' He laughed in ridicule, and said, 'Very well, have your own way; but before going, take off that *hansli*' (a thick silver collar worn as an ornament), 'and bring out your jewels, for they are my property.'

All who know anything about Indian women will be aware how much they value and prize their jewels;

tinkling as they go, they form no small attraction to the feminine mind. But Bhaktin was equal to the occasion, and passed through the trial without flinching. Without a word, she placed them all at her brother's feet. Widows as a rule wear no jewels. Bhaktin had only a thick silver collar, worn as an ornament, which she took off. Her other jewels were kept in the house, and these she brought forward, and put them before her brother.

On seeing her do this, Bálá, the child of his first wife, rushed into Bhaktin's arms and began to cry. Bhaktin loved this child as her own soul, and petted him very much. Taking him into her arms, she said to her brother, 'Let this child go with me, for since his mother died he has been a son to me.' But the brother tore away the boy from her arms, and said fiercely, 'You shall not take the child; get out of my house quickly.' Bhaktin heaved a deep sigh, and burst into tears, and left the house weeping as if her heart would break. On hearing her cries, Bálá burst into a flood of tears, and the other children also began to scream and call out, 'Come back, aunty! come back to us, aunty!' Her sister-in-law also besought her to return, for they all loved her very much.

Bhaktin was very much exercised in mind what to do. She, however, overcame her feelings of natural affection in the stern sense of duty to God, and proceeded to the house of prayer with a sad heart. When the service was ended, she told the whole story to the brethren. Babu Hira Lall and Dharmdás went to see her brother, to explain to him the motives from which she had acted, and endeavoured to show him how wrong it was thus to treat his widowed sister. 'Do not treat your sister in this way,' they said, 'but receive her back into your house, and avoid a scandal amongst your neighbours by such conduct.' But he refused to comply with their request, and said, 'If she makes up her mind to put away this nonsense, I will receive her again; otherwise, I will not allow her to darken my door.'

When the brethren saw it was useless talking to him any longer, they left the house, and arranged amongst themselves that for the present she should live with Premdás' mother. They thought her brother would relent in a day or two, and call her back again of his own free will. But two weeks passed away, and her brother's anger showed no signs of abating. If he ever by accident met her in the road, he turned his face another way, and took no notice of her. At last the brethren and Premdás, seeing how things were turning out, decided to help her to build a little hut of her own. One of Premdás' houses, which had been burnt down during that terrible trial of his, had not been rebuilt; so he gave Bhaktin that piece of land on which to build a small house, and said to her, 'Sister, fear not; the Lord will take care of you. Build a house, and my mother will live with you.'

Our readers should know that Premdás' wife had died some time before, and he was a widower. He had no one living with him but his younger brother and his mother. Bhaktin readily built herself a grass hut, and the brethren most willingly put the thatch on for her. When all was ready, and the house covered with cow-dung as a plastering, according to native fashion, and her small mud fireplace for cooking was in readiness, it so happened that Babu Hira Lall paid his usual visit to Phulkiya, to conduct Sunday service. Bhaktin, hearing his voice, came out of her hut with great ceremony, and besought him to bless the widow's house with his presence. She desired the feet of her teacher to tread its precincts, humble as it was, before any one else; for she felt sure he would bring a blessing with him. 'Remain,' she said, 'in this widow's house till you return home, and I will cook your food in my new fireplace; for I shall consider it a great favour if you will honour my house with your presence.'

Babu Hira Lall was an old man, and on receiving this invitation he entered her grass hut. Bhaktin was so delighted at this time, she felt as if all the blessings of the world were hers. The Babu called Premdás and his young brother, and said, 'Come, let us ask a blessing on this new home.' And so they prayed for Bhaktin, and asked the Lord to take care of this dear sister, who had been turned out of house and home for Christ's sake. When the prayer was ended, Bhaktin, with eyes full of tears, said, 'It is enough; my heart has received comfort. Yes, my people have turned me out of doors for the sake of Jesus Christ, but the Lord has taken me up. Now there is no hindrance, I will be baptized, and become a handmaiden of the Lord Jesus.'

CHAPTER XI.

JETHÚ'S WIFE BROUGHT TO THE LORD.

ONE Sunday, Babu Hira Lall went to see Jethú Mandal, and found him alone; his wife and children had gone to see some friends. As the catechist began to speak to Jethú, the latter despondingly said, 'How shall I endure all this? I am afraid my wife will run away again. I bear with patience all that is said to me, but I am only flesh and blood, and my heart is sorely tried. I feel sometimes as if my heart would break.' Having said this, he burst into tears. The catechist, seeing his distress, was filled with pity for poor Jethú. With great affection and love he tried to comfort him, and give him encouragement for the future, saying, 'Brother, only take your trouble to the Lord Jesus. It is no use expecting your wife to understand; you have already tried your best, but it is of no avail; you must now fall into the hands of the Lord. Bring your trials and sorrows to Him in prayer, and He will have mercy upon you. Ask Him to soften the heart of your wife, and open her eyes to see Jesus as her Lord and Saviour. In answer to prayer, her temper and spirit will undergo a change, and she will understand all you have in vain tried to teach her. Yes, brother, you have prayed for her, I know, but do not grow weary; a blessing will follow, and God will indeed hear you. Let us kneel down now, and call upon the Lord for this purpose.'

Both of them knelt down on the bare ground, and the catechist began very earnestly to pray, and wept as he prayed. During the prayer his heart was warmed more and more, and he waxed more and more importunate, and with great boldness and faith he wrestled with God in prayer. Like Jacob of old, he said, 'I will not let Thee go unless Thou bless her.' As they were praying, they heard Jethú's wife coming through the village towards the house, storming and grumbling. She came and sat down in the enclosure before the hut, making a terrible noise; but the catechist heeded her not, but went on praying.

After a time her boisterous spirit was somewhat subdued, and she began to listen to the catechist praying and weeping in supplication before God. Suddenly, while the prayer was going on, she rushed into the hut, and, sitting down on the ground, began to weep bitterly. The catechist rose from his knees, and the sobbing woman cried out, 'I have sinned! Forgive me, forgive me! For a long time I have been convinced that the Lord Jesus is the only true Saviour. Satan has tempted me to oppose my convictions, and prevented me from repenting of my sins. Now I repent in dust and ashes. May the Lord have mercy on my soul!' She sobbed and wept so loud that she was unable to speak.

Jethú, seeing her great distress, burst into a flood of tears, and wept so long and loud that both the catechist and his wife thought he would bring on some internal injury by his violent distress, and they tried hard to comfort him. They did not know that, on seeing his wife's tender spirit of sorrow, he wept for joy.

As this scene was going on, all the Satguruwás who lived near them had heard the terrible weeping in Jethú's house, and ran to see what was the matter. When Jethú's wife saw the people crowd into the hut, she ran into the cow-shed and hid herself, and wept alone. Bhaktin, however, followed her, and tried to speak a few words of consolation. After a little conversation, Babu Hira Lall said, with great thankfulness, 'Brothers, let us offer thanksgiving to the Giver of all good things for the mercies of to-day. Truly hath the Lord said, "And it shall come to pass, that before they call, I will answer; and while they are yet speaking, I will hear."'[1] From that day Jethú's wife believed on the Lord Jesus with all her heart, and husband and wife were of one mind and of one soul in this matter.

About that time the news reached Tulsiya, in her father-in-law's house, that several disciples of the Bábá-Jí had become Christians, and that Bhaktin was one of them; but this was not true, for Bhaktin was not yet baptized. Tulsiya did not know that her aunt had been turned out of doors by her father, nor did she know anything of what had been going on among the Satguruwás. When she heard the news that some of them had become Christians, she grew very impatient, and said in her heart that she could not endure the persecutions of her father-in-law much longer. She saw but one way out of her difficulties, namely, by giving up caste, and becoming a Christian; for she felt sure in such a case he would turn her out of doors.

She knew her father-in-law would never allow her to return to Phulkiya, so she set about scheming how she

[1] Isa. lxv. 24.

could arrange to run away. She made an arrangement with an old widow woman to aid her in getting away, and to go with her to Phulkiya. The woman agreed; and forthwith, on that very night, she escaped from her father-in-law's house.

As soon as the unfortunate girl reached her father's house, she became aware that he had turned her aunt out of the house, and that he was more than ever incensed against Christianity. Her father immediately locked Tulsiya in a room, and refused to allow her to leave it. She cried very much, and said, 'Let me go to my aunt, or else send for her to see me;' but he was inexorable. Her father-in-law followed her to Phulkiya, and at once her father made her over to him. She, poor creature! was caught in her own net; she knew that now she would be punished and persecuted more than ever; for she had given her father-in-law just reason to be angry with her. But Tulsiya did not trouble herself much with forebodings; she rather turned it over in her own mind how she could become a Christian, and thus put an end to this uncertainty. She knew her father-in-law would now make such arrangements as to prevent her running away again.

Tulsiya's father was very much exercised in mind about his daughter's determination to become a Christian. He saw she would in no wise give up her intention, but he was very solicitous to put an end to this state of uncertainty in his house. He was angry that neither his sister nor his daughter would listen to him on this subject.

When Tulsiya's father-in-law was taking her away from Phulkiya, her father rebuked her severely, and said, 'When will you put an end to this stupid opposition? You bring all this punishment on yourself, and you well deserve it.' Tulsiya, nothing daunted, replied, 'I shall never change my mind on this subject. You may kill me if you like, it will be all the same; do what you like.'

As Tulsiya was leaving the village, she cast a glance towards the mound on which Premdás' house stood, and there she saw her aunt standing looking at her. Tulsiya wrung her hands, called out, wept aloud; but her father-in-law pushed her forcibly on, and refused to allow her to say one word. Impelled by fear, she continued her journey, but now and then looking behind her and calling her aunt by name. Poor, helpless Bhaktin looked on in great grief; she could do nothing.

When Tulsiya had disappeared in the dim distance, Bhaktin smote her breast, and said, 'O Lord God, do Thou make a way for her to escape!'

CHAPTER XII.

THE LORD MANIFESTS HIS POWER.

AN outside observer would have thought that the work of the Lord was scarcely going on in Phulkiya, but in reality it was not so. God has many ways by which He can draw men to Himself; sometimes it is by blessing, sometimes by sorrow; sometimes when men are enjoying peace and rest, and sometimes by fear and terror. He brings His erring children by many ways into the right path. The Satguruwás, whom He had drawn in some measure towards Himself, He influenced by a most wonderful circumstance. This happened suddenly in Phulkiya, and many of them were ready and prepared by it to become Christians.

It happened on this wise. There was in Phulkiya a Satguruwá who was more zealous than all the rest in the religion of the Bábá-Jí, but after some years, when the Brahmins persecuted the Satguruwás, this man, being very much troubled by them, was weak enough to yield to their solicitations, and he began to worship idols again. From that time he became the greatest enemy of the Satguruwás. He persecuted them even more than the Brahmins did, in order to make them Hindus like himself; for he desired to wipe out the name of the Bábá-Jí's religion from the village.

The previous year the missionary had paid a visit to his house, and asked him why he persecuted the Satguruwás so much; what harm had they done him? 'You yourself,' said he, 'were once on the right way—why are you in the mire again? Turn to the Lord, and repent of this great sin. He will forgive you, and wash away your sin.' But this man would not listen, and he continued to persecute the disciples of the Bábá-Jí as much as ever.

When Dharmdás and the other two Satguruwás were baptized, this man was taken ill, and in August he was so ill that his relatives despaired of his life. In this state, he began to be very much afraid, and wondered what would become of him if he died, and where he would go. He was now very sorry he had given up the truth, and for worldly peace and pleasure endangered his immortal soul. One day, when he was in great anxiety of mind and body, he said to his wife, 'I have committed a great sin; go quickly and call Dharmdás or some other Christian; I want to say something to him.'

But Dharmdás and the two other Christians had gone to the fair to buy cattle. Then he sent for poor afflicted Jethú, but he was so ill at the time that he was unable to move. When he heard the Christians were away, and that Jethú was too ill to come, he became more and more distressed in mind, and called for Bhaktin, saying, 'She is almost as good as a real Christian, and if she cannot come, call the catechist from Sáhibganj; for the terrors of my heart nearly eat me up.'

Fortunately Bhaktin was at home. When she came to see him, he smote his breast and said, 'Dear sister, my heart is very troubled. Why did I persecute you all? Your religion is true, and you are on the way to eternal life. Oh, sister, forgive my waywardness, and let me now hear something about religion. The missionary and the catechist took a good deal of trouble to explain things to me, but I would not listen, and shut my ears to the truth; I did not treasure up what they said to me.'

Bhaktin gave him all the comfort she could, and explained to him all she knew. She sat by him all that night, and ministered to his wants and necessities; but his fear and terror continued to increase, and in the pains of death he cried out and trembled. The next day he said, 'I shall to-day go to destruction, for I deserve eternal death!'

Bhaktin tried to bring light to his heart, but he received no comfort. When the pains of death were upon him, all cried out in fear, for they thought him dead. They smote their breasts, and prepared to carry his body to the river Ganges, but after a short time he opened his eyes and heaved a deep sigh. After two hours the death-rattle again set in, but he recovered again after an hour, but was so weak that he was unable to speak. In the middle of the night he swooned again, and again they prepared to carry his body to the Ganges, but all at once he opened his eyes and became sensible. He made a sign to Bhaktin, who was sitting near him. She asked him what he wished to say. 'You have been dying,' she said, 'and are still alive. Three times you appeared to be dead, and three times your life has been given to you again. What has happened to you?'

The man breathed a deep sigh, and, though he was almost unable to speak, he very slowly, resting after each word, said, 'What can I do? My soul was going to hell;

it was dark all round. I was afraid; I could not linger there. O God, what shall I do? How can I die thus?' Having said so much, he began to cry, and then said suddenly, 'I have found one way out of the difficulty; I see how I can receive comfort and die in peace. Sister,' said he to Bhaktin, 'take my brass vessel, and wash it with your own hands, and take away with your hands its idolatrous impurity, then draw some water from Premdás' well. I will take water from your hands, for you are a Christian in heart, and then I can die in peace.'

His wife and children were so filled with awe and fear that they could not forbid this act, although they knew his caste would be taken away by it. Bhaktin ran and washed the vessel, and brought some water from the Christians' well. When the sick man saw it, he seized the vessel with both hands, but from sheer weakness he could not lift it up. His mother assisted, and Bhaktin gave him to drink. When he had drunk the water, and was giving the vessel back again, he said, 'It is enough; I have given up caste and idolatry.' Turning to his father and mother and wife, he added, 'Take care that you all become Christians, and that my children are taught that holy religion. Then, when you come to die, your end will be peace, and you will not have to fear as I have had.'

Then he lay down upon his bed and fell asleep, and this was his last sleep. In the evening they burned his body, according to the custom of the Hindus, and threw the ashes into the river Ganges.

CHAPTER XIII.

THE LORD'S WAY MADE MANIFEST.

THE hearts of all the Satguruwás were filled with fear when they heard of the strange death-scene just described, and they continued in a state of restlessness, and said one to another, 'What does all this mean? Some evil spirit must have possessed him which would not allow him to die in peace. But how was it that when Bhaktin gave him water to drink from the Christians' well, and his caste was broken, he died in apparent peace and comfort? What will happen to us when we come to die?'

At last, after much anxious thought, the Satguruwás decided it would be better for them to become Christians, because they could see no safe way of escape from eternal death but this. They were afraid that if they did not accept the Gospel of Christ, the anger of the Lord would fall upon them, and evil spirits take possession of them, and give them no peace.

One of the Satguruwás went to Sáhibganj to visit Babu Hira Lall, and told him the story of the terrible death of this man, and, folding his hands before him after the Indian fashion, besought him to come speedily and prepare the Satguruwás who were willing to be taught for baptism, 'lest,' as he said, 'when death comes to us, we should fall into the same fear and dread.'

The Babu, after hearing the whole story, praised God, and said, 'The hand of the Lord is not shortened that He cannot save. With Him nothing is difficult, nothing is impossible; for He can save to the uttermost those who come unto God by Him. When nothing apparently follows the teaching of His servants, He can use the enemies of the Gospel to magnify His name, and carry out His great designs. Blessed be God! You remember how the missionary and I explained to you all these things, but you refused to listen to and believe the Gospel. Now the Lord is drawing you to Himself through one who was an enemy of the Gospel, from amongst yourselves. Praised be the Lord, who has had mercy on you, and turned your steps towards the fold of Christ! God grant that you may remain firm in this state of mind, and not turn again like a sow to her wallowing in the mire!'

The catechist returned with the man to Phulkiya, and arranged to remain amongst them for a month, to teach them as opportunity occurred, and to prepare them for baptism, so that when the missionary came they might be received into the Christian Church without further delay.

When Dharmdás, Premdás, and that other Christian returned from the fair where they had gone to buy cattle, and heard the heart-rending story of this terrible death, they were indeed very much astonished, and praised the Lord, who had done such wonderful things in their midst. 'Now,' they said, 'there will not only be three Christian families in Phulkiya, but when these Satguruwás become Christians there will be a congregation of fifty souls in our village.'

There was a fair number of inquirers, namely, Bhaktin and her brother, with all his family; Jethú and his wife; the father and mother, wife and children of the man whose death had read them such a terrible lesson; all these and others continued to receive instruction, day and night, in the scriptural truths which a Christian ought to know and accept to the saving of his soul.

To these things they gave their undivided attention during this season of preparation. They sang Christian hymns, and continued instant in prayer. Their zeal for instruction put such a tax upon the energies of Babu Hira Lall, that he was obliged to redouble his efforts to meet their demands for instruction, and he soon fell ill, and was obliged to return to Sáhibganj. The missionary, hearing of his illness, sent another brother to carry on the work of preparation, so that the work of the Lord should not be hindered.

Wonderful to relate, the Hindus of Phulkiya said nothing to all this going on under their eyes. They knew now that all their scheming to hinder the progress of the Gospel was of no avail, and that the Satguruwás would become Christians. In fact, they confessed that the Christians had conquered. They were now silent, and gave the inquirers no trouble.

The news of this sudden change amongst the Satguruwás reached Tulsiya's village, and her husband's people heard that her father, with all his family, was going to join the Christian Church, and that he had called his sister Bhaktin home again. They watched Tulsiya more closely than before, lest she should run away again. It happened, however, one day, that the family went to make some purchases in a village a few miles away, and only her father-in-law was left to take care of her, and look after the house. About noon he retired to one corner of the room to take his siesta, and soon fell asleep; Tulsiya, finding a good opportunity, fled from the house, and reached her father's home the day after in safety.

On reaching Phulkiya, she soon became aware of the events which had taken place lately. All was true that she had heard. When she saw her aunt, she fell on her neck and wept, and through fear turned her face away from her father, only now and then casting a glance towards him. His heart, she saw, by the grace of God, was changed, and he received her with every sign of love and affection. When all had welcomed her, and the family sat down to consider if they could safely allow her to remain in the house, the persecutor of this poor girl arrived, and presented himself before the door.

When Tulsiya heard the sound of her father-in-law's voice, she set up a fearful scream, and fell at her father's feet, and cried out, 'Do not send me back with him; he will kill me!' When her people heard her fearful cries, and saw her beating her breast in terror, falling upon the ground and beating her head against the floor, they indeed pitied her very much, and, in their confusion, one advised one thing and one another. Her father-in-law abused her soundly in not very polite language, and attempted to kick his daughter-in-law, where she had fallen at her father's feet in fear and terror.

The people of the village, hearing the noise, rushed to see what was taking place, and they laughed at Tulsiya in derision, and began to move the father-in-law to press his claim more vigorously. 'She is your daughter-in-law,' they said, 'and ought to obey your wishes. Be sure and take her home again, otherwise she will become a Christian.'

At last her father, seeing how helpless they all were in the matter, said to Tulsiya, 'We cannot do anything for you; you must return with your father-in-law. Trust in the Lord, and He will arrange for you, my child.'

Tulsiya saw that all her weeping was useless; it was her duty to return with her father-in-law. She also now noticed the people laughing and scoffing, and out of a sense of shame she became silent, and ran into her stepmother's room, thoroughly ashamed of herself. When the people had gone away, and things had quieted down, she no longer refused to return. She took leave of her family, and, thoroughly broken in spirit, she followed her father-in-law home, weeping all the way.

On reaching her destination, the sorrows and trials of this poor creature were redoubled. Her mother-in-law took off her jewels, clothed her in rough garments, bound her with a strong rope, and confined her to the house, saying, 'Will you go there again?'

Tulsiya had endured all in silence, but, when she was bound with a rope, she said, 'I am not a bullock or a cow, which you can bind and confine all its life; when I get loose, I shall run away and become a Christian.'

The time she passed in this state of confinement told upon her health. Through sorrow and trouble her sleep and appetite forsook her, and each day she became weaker and weaker. When her relatives saw how weak and ill she had become, they released her from confinement, and, much to their astonishment, she did not attempt to run away. One reason was, she was too weak to attempt a journey of a day and a half; another was, she had decided in her own mind that when she heard that the missionary had come to Phulkiya, she would run away, and ask her father to break her caste, give her food to eat and water to drink, for she knew her father-in-law could not have her in the house if she became a Christian.

After deciding this in her own mind, Tulsiya began to dwell in peace, and as she went about her daily avocations as usual her health steadily improved. Her father-in-law's people saw her apparently settling down, and they foolishly thought she had made up her mind to make the best of a bad case, and spend her days with them. They began, therefore, to treat her more leniently, and show her signs of affection. The subject of religion was never referred to.

CHAPTER XIV.

THE DAY OF TRIAL AND THE DAY OF BLESSING.

ON account of pressure of other work, the missionary could not visit Phulkiya till the end of January. Then, however, news reached Tulsiya's village that he was coming to Phulkiya. This news brought joy to Tulsiya's heart, and she began to consider how she could run off again, and be released from her life of imprisonment; for such it was even now. For ten days she sought an opportunity to accomplish her design, but she was closely watched. At last, when all were asleep one night, the opportunity presented itself, and she ran away.

On a previous occasion, it will be remembered, she had secured the assistance of an old labouring widow woman who accompanied her home. But this time the woman would not listen to her entreaties, but said, 'If I accompany you, and this thing should become known to your father-in-law, who knows what he will do to me? I cannot help you.' Tulsiya was obliged, therefore, to proceed on her journey alone. The poor creature was very weak and ill, but dare not rest anywhere on the way, lest her father-in-law should overtake her.

She at last reached Phulkiya—weak, tired, and footsore.

When her father, mother, and aunt saw Tulsiya, and observed how weak and faint she had become through long endurance and fretting, looking withered and pinched, their hearts went out towards her, and they began to feel anxious for the child. She narrated to them all she had suffered, and they determined to take a decided step, and gave her food to eat and water to drink from their own vessels. In India this means a great deal, where the caste question stands in the way. Tulsiya's caste was now broken, and she was comforted, and said, 'My father-in-law would not now take me back if I wished to go.'

After some hours, the father-in-law appeared with his neighbours, bringing a strong rope with him to bind her, and shoes with which to beat her. It is the greatest indignity possible to beat a person with a shoe in India. He came foaming with rage; but Tulsiya sat in the house fearless, knowing full well that matters were now changed between them. When her father-in-law heard that she had eaten and drunk water in the house, he was like a madman with rage. But what was the use of getting into a rage now? She had broken her caste, and slipped from his iron grasp, for he could not allow her to eat and drink with his family again. Having made many boasting remarks, he said, 'Very well; this girl is now dead to me and mine, and I shall marry my son to some one else.' Having delivered himself on this wise, he took his departure.

It so happened that on the very day Tulsiya reached home, in the evening the missionary and his daughter came to Phulkiya; but they knew nothing of her story. She began to receive instruction, with a view to baptism, along with her father, mother, and aunt.

The Satguruwás passed about two months in untold happiness; for in the same measure as they were taught with love and zeal, in the same degree they gave themselves, heart and soul, to be instructed and taught. Amongst all the inquirers, Tulsiya and her aunt were the most sincere. When the love of the Saviour for the sons of men was touchingly described, their hearts were filled with love and joy, and tears started in their eyes.

Babu Hira Lall, who had fallen ill during the rains, was taken worse, and showed no signs of final recovery. But when he heard, at the end of the cold season, that a date had been fixed for the baptism of the Satguruwás, he was very anxious to visit Phulkiya, and see the disciples of the Bábá-Jí received into the Christian Church. The missionary strongly advised him not to leave his home in such a weak state of health, and his wife and children also besought him to stay at home; but he would listen to none of them. His soul was bound up in this beloved work, and he determined to come and to carry out the desire of his heart, whatever God was pleased to send. When he heard that the baptisms would take place on the following Sunday, he ordered a bullock-cart, and with the help of the brethren he was placed on it, and then, ordering the driver to proceed, said, 'I must see the baptism of these people, and then, O Lord, like Simeon of old, "let Thy servant depart in peace, for mine eyes have seen Thy salvation!"'

This man of God, weak and ill, reached Phulkiya safely. On the Sunday morning, when the disciples of the Bábá-Jí were proceeding to bathe before attending divine service, their old teacher and preacher cut off from each the sacred lock of hair, which they had continued to wear up to this time. This sacred lock is the badge of Hinduism, which, up to that time, although they were Satguruwás, they had continued to protect. This is generally the last step before baptism, and entails great self-denial and resolution on the part of the inquirer. This small amount of labour was too much for Babu Hira Lall, and he fell into a deadly swoon. When the hour for divine service arrived, he lay senseless on the ground, and the Satguruwás were obliged to proceed alone to the service; their teacher could not accompany them. The missionary had provided for the services a large tent, in order to accommodate a large number. It was evidently a great tax on the resources of Dharmdás to clean out his cow-shed every Sunday for divine service.

Early in the morning all the people in the villages around Phulkiya (for the news had spread quickly and far) assembled to witness this strange ceremony, for it was entirely new to them. They were curious to see how the Satguruwás would be made Christians. At first the people remained very quiet, but when the baptismal service commenced they began to talk and make a great noise and confusion. In their anger they made use of abusive language, and began to curse, laugh, and scoff. Some one called out, 'Set the tent on fire, and stop the service.' Another said, 'Pull down the tent, and put an end to this nonsense.'

The disciples of the Bábá-Jí, on hearing their abusive threats, were dreadfully afraid, and their wives and daughters wished to run away, for they had made up their minds that the people of the village would never allow the ceremony to take place, and would do something to hinder them from being baptized. When the congregation inside the tent heard the uproar and confusion without, they were unable to give their minds to the service which was proceeding. If the missionary had shown the least sign of wavering or fear, then indeed the service would have been brought to a close, for the disciples of the Bábá-Jí were ready to run away; but when they saw him proceed with the service without the least sign of fear, in spite of the noise and confusion created by the enemies of the Gospel, then these new disciples of Jesus gained courage, and sat down and gave their minds to the service. When the crowd saw that none of them were afraid, they too became silent.

Of the new converts, Bhaktin and Tulsiya seemed the happiest. When the service was over, and the missionary's daughter shook hands with Bhaktin, the dear old widow said, 'After all the sorrows and cares I have passed through, the Lord has allowed me to see this day, and obtain the desire of my heart. I am comforted now, and my heart is at rest. Truly we are happy, and the soul is satisfied when Jesus dwells in us and abides with us.'

CHAPTER XV.

'BLESSED ARE THE DEAD WHICH DIE IN THE LORD.'

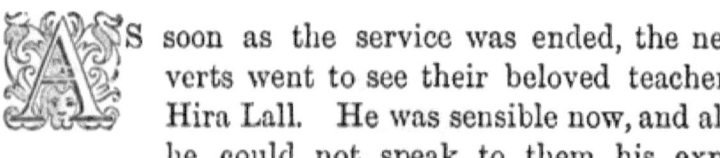S soon as the service was ended, the new converts went to see their beloved teacher, Babu Hira Lall. He was sensible now, and although he could not speak to them his expression was one of supreme happiness and joy. He made a sign to them all to sit down. When they were seated, he folded his hands in prayer, and looking towards heaven, his soul was engaged in prayer for some time. Although this devoted servant could not speak, from the movements of his lips it was manifest he was thanking the Lord for the mercies of that day. On seeing him thus engaged, all the new converts knelt down and thanked the Lord for all He had done through His servant.

In the evening the converts went to the missionary's tent, and talked with him. They recounted all the difficulties, sorrows, and trials which the disciples of the Bábá-Jí had passed through when they gave up the worship of the Hindu gods, and began to call, in their imperfect way, on the name of the Lord. It was then fifteen years since the original Bábá-Jí came to the village, and about one hundred and fifty families had joined this new religion. Of those, fifty persons had now become Christians; some had left the village, and the rest had gone back to heathenism.

The missionary was very sorry that the Faqír had not been seen in the village for a long time, because he thought possibly he might know something more about the original Bábá-Jí. His uncle, who was his follower, would surely have told more of this strange visitor. Where did he get the copy of The Lamp of Wisdom, with which he allured the people to the Gospel of Christ? Was he a Christian, who in this peculiar form was spreading the knowledge of the Gospel of Christ? Or was he really a Hindu Faqír, who recognised the religion taught in the *Gyándípak* as God's eternal truth? Possibly it will never be known in this world, but one day it will be known who this man was who in this curious way laid the foundation of the Lord's work, and through whose indirect instrumentality fifty people had been received into the Christian Church.

The day after the baptisms, Babu Hira Lall returned home, and that very week the Lord called His servant up higher—released him from his pain and sickness, and exalted him to that home where sorrow and weariness flee away. Yes, blessed are the dead which die in the Lord.

The missionary purchased the small house which had been built for Bhaktin in Premdás' courtyard when her brother turned her out of house and home. It was no longer required, for Bhaktin had returned to her brother's house. This house was given to the new catechist who had taken Hira Lall's place, and who was appointed to minister to the spiritual wants of the Phulkiya Christians. The missionary then returned to Bhágalpur, as the hot season was coming on apace; and the disciples of the

Bábá-Jí, who had been persecuted so long by the people around them, now began to pass their days in peace and safety, and were very happy.

When they became Christians their Hindu friends broke off all intercourse with them, and those who lived near left that part of the village, and made themselves houses on the north side of the village, a little distance off, and called their part Rámgarh, namely, Rám's stronghold, because they would only own Rám as their god, and at that distance they would be unable to hear Christian hymns and prayers. That part of Phulkiya where the Christians lived was called by the Hindus Isáítola, namely, village of Jesusites, or Christian village.

Tulsiya's father, mother, and aunt were very much exercised in mind what to do for her; they were afraid that she would have to live all her life like a widow, in sorrow and trouble, and this was indeed a trial to them; for they could not entertain the idea of marrying her to some one else. They wished somehow to influence her husband, who was now a young man eighteen years of age, and thus bring them together again. They knew he was very fond of Tulsiya, for he had never joined the others in persecuting his young wife, and had shown in every way an affection for her. They also heard that he had refused to contract another marriage, which proved to Tulsiya's family that his heart was bound up with the girl. They hoped that he would gradually come to Christ, and agree with them about the Christian religion.

They tried to induce his relatives and friends to persuade him to come to his wife, but all their endeavours proved fruitless. Although the young man was no enemy of the Christians, he was not willing to leave his father's house and home, even for his wife. He was the youngest and beloved son of his parents. They never rebuked or reproved him for anything, and he passed his time at home as a thoroughly lazy young man. He ate, drank, slept, and did just what he wished. The young man knew if he went to his father-in-law's house he would certainly have to work like other men, and the idea of this was quite enough to deter him from joining his wife. 'I shall have to work,' he said, 'and obey my father-in-law, and do all he tells me. If I become a Christian I shall have to give up the worship of idols, and all the fun and excitement attending therefrom, and there will be no happiness for me.' One day a Christian from Phulkiya met him, and tried to persuade him to think about the salvation of his soul; but his reply was, 'Who knows anything about the future? Who knows whether all this is true?'

All this was reported to Tulsiya's people, and made them nearly hopeless; for they knew not what to do in this emergency. One day, Tulsiya's aunt was thinking over the turn things had taken, and suddenly an idea entered her mind as if an inspiration. She called her brother and his wife at once, and said, 'We have tried everything but one, and the most important one we have forgotten. We have never made the matter a special subject of prayer, and how can we expect things to come right unless we ask the Lord most earnestly? We ought to beseech the Lord, and ask Him to help us in this difficulty, and show us what to do and what not to do. Cannot He arrange for this dear child? Let us pray specially each day for this purpose, and He will help us.'

Both her brother and his wife were delighted with the suggestion, and they appointed a time each day to pray for guidance and help, and from that day they never relaxed their energies, but sought at the throne of grace the guidance they sorely needed.

Several months passed away, and nothing occurred to point out the way. It is sometimes the Lord's will to try the faith of His servants, and strengthen them by refusing to give for a time an answer to their prayers, and so they were left to pray and wait the development of the providence of God.

At last another rainy season passed, and the missionary came again to Phulkiya. Bhaktin told his daughter all that had passed in their family. 'This is our trouble now,' she said, 'and this is the way we have asked the Lord to help us.' She was comforted, and told to go on praying, and trust in the Lord for guidance. 'Whatever is for Tulsiya's good,' said the missionary's daughter, 'He will carry out, and He will open the way Himself for the future.' Bhaktin, with eyes full of tears, could only answer, 'Yes, we are doing this; we shall not give up praying. If He does not help us, who will?'

CHAPTER XVI.

THE SEEDS OF CASTE STILL LINGER.

SOME years before this part of our story, the wife of Premdás had died, and his mother, who did the work of the house, was getting old and weak. Premdás therefore determined to marry again; but there was no one in the village amongst the Christians suitable for a wife. He naturally mentioned his wish to the missionary, and asked his advice. The missionary said, 'I see it is impossible for you to find a wife amongst our own people, and therefore I am of the opinion that you should marry one of the orphan girls from the Orphanage in Bhágalpur. I will select a girl for you who is good and religious; she will be able to read and write also. If she is pleased to come here and live with you and be your wife, and you are satisfied also, then arrangements for the marriage will be made. She will be able to teach her sisters in the village to sew, knit, read and write, and, it is to be hoped, will prove a real help and blessing to the Christians of Phulkiya.'

Premdás highly approved of the suggestion; but when he told Dharmdás and the brethren what arrangements were going to be made for him, they were all very angry, and said, 'Are you going to bring some unknown woman in our midst, about whose antecedents we know nothing? Who knows what caste she may have sprung from? We cannot agree to this arrangement.' The missionary and the catechist showed the Christians how wrong it was to bring forth such objections now they were Christians—that their idea was contrary to the Word of God and the spirit of the Gospel. 'If Premdás is willing,' they said, 'and the girl is worthy of him, then you should put no obstacle in his way of contracting this lawful and desirable marriage. Have you become Hindus again, and do you observe caste? Christians have for ever cast all these things behind them.'

But the Christians were not convinced, and they forbade Premdás to bring any such girl to the village, refusing to acknowledge her. They advised him to marry from amongst his own people, or remain a widower.

Premdás, hearing this decision from his Christian brethren, was very much in doubt how to act, and knew not what to do. He endeavoured to banish the idea of marrying from his mind; but the missionary would not allow the matter to end in this way. He explained to the village Puncháyat and Dharmdás why this rule could not be retained amongst Christians. At last, after some weeks, they gave way, and said Premdás could marry whom he wished, and they would put no obstacle in the way. Although they gave permission for the marriage to take place, it was evident they only gave way out of a feeling of policy, and not from conviction. The pride of caste in a measure still ruled their hearts.

Premdás, on receiving this permission from the village committee, went to Bhágalpur, and selected his future bride. The girl was willing; so arrangements were made for the marriage. The missionary advised them to have the marriage ceremony in Phulkiya before all the Christians. When the time arrived, the missionary sent the girl for a couple of weeks to the house of a Christian near Phulkiya, in order that the names of the bride and bridegroom might be called in the Christian congregation, and all should know the Christian custom of marriage. The brethren saw they could not prevent the marriage taking place, yet in their hearts they were very angry. They heard the scoffs and sneers of the heathen in the village, and their curses were again freely flung at the Christians. 'Who knows,' said they, 'what low caste woman will now come amongst these Christians?' The old feeling of hatred against the Christians was revived, and the Christians had again to endure much persecution.

The state of things had reached such a pitch, and the pressure brought to bear upon the Christians in this instance was so great, that when the wedding-day arrived, and the missionary's daughter brought the bride from the village where she was staying, none of the Christians wished to attend the ceremony. The catechist rebuked them severely for their behaviour towards Premdás and his future wife. They were somewhat ashamed of themselves after what the catechist had said to them, and when they saw the other people of the village, old and young, male and female, collect near the missionary's tent to see the marriage ceremony, they also went to witness it; but they altogether refused to take any of the refreshments provided for them, and returned to their homes after the ceremony.

Premdás was very much grieved, for he had made arrangements for a dinner, and invited them; but only Bhaktin and Tulsiya came. He sat, grieved and sorrowful, in his house; and the poor girl wept sorely on seeing the treatment they had received from the Christians. Although Bhaktin and Premdás' mother were very much grieved, they tried to comfort the bride; but indeed this was no day of happiness, but one of sorrow and grief. When Premdás saw that none of his brethren, save Bhaktin and Tulsiya, were coming to the dinner, he sent each some uncooked meat and food, which they willingly took; but Dharmdas refused to accept his share, and returned it, saying, 'I shall have nothing whatever to do with Premdás. He refused to listen to the village committee; let him take the consequences. He has opposed our wish, and see what persecution we have had to endure on his account, and what will follow we know not yet.'

The missionary and his daughter went to see the bride and the bridegroom. They found them in great distress of mind; but the missionary said to them, 'Do not be at all afraid, nor grieved in any way. God, the Almighty Father, will bless you, and dwell with you always. You have entered into this marriage agreement in the name of the Lord Jesus, and He will never forsake you. If He help and support you, and other people trouble you, what does it matter? Your Christian brethren are troubling and grieving you, in ignorance of the spirit of the Gospel; but you will see that, through the grace of God, they will all be your warm friends before long.'

This state of opposition continued for a couple of weeks; but when they saw that Premdás' bride was humble and kind, their anger gradually began to abate. In truth, Mohini was a thoroughly religious and good girl. She learned to love her mother-in-law, and was quite obedient to her. She did all the work of the house in a womanly way; and when her mother-in-law used to say to her that she was a bride, and should not work yet, she would laughingly reply, 'Mother, you are growing old, and you should now take rest, and pass your days in comfort. Let me do the work of the house.'

When the anger of the brethren had altogether abated, they began to visit her. She received them all tenderly and lovingly; so that instead of hating her they all began to love her most dearly. The women and children came to her regularly, and learned to sew and read. In this way the Lord led His servants from the paths of superstition and prejudice to the paths of peace and knowledge.

CHAPTER XVII.

BHAKTIN LEARNS TO READ HER BIBLE.

BHAKTIN loved Mohini very much, and praised her to every one, because she could not only read and write, but do the work of the house; and what she did not know of housework she willingly learned from her mother-in-law. 'She was not lazy, like many silly women,' she would say; 'she would not pass her spare time in gossiping and smoking, and eating all kinds of rubbish; but she is active, spending her spare moments in reading, or writing to her old friends at the Orphanage. We are all very ignorant indeed,' Bhaktin said; 'but we should learn a lesson, and teach our daughters and daughters-in-law to imitate Mohini.'

Bhaktin would often sit near Mohini, and ask her to read to her from the Word of God. When she heard the beautiful stories from the Bible, and its words of comfort sounded in her ears, her heart was filled with emotion, and she was never tired of hearing the old, old story of the cross.

One day Bhaktin said, 'I wish I could read; then I would read the Word of God day and night.' She repeated this wish on different occasions; but suddenly, one day, coming to a final decision, she said, 'I will learn to read. I will go now and ask the missionary's daughter to let me have the First Hindi Reading-Book. You must teach me, dear Mohini. Why should I not learn to read?'

So saying, she ran off to the missionary's daughter, who, on hearing her request, was very doubtful of the issue. She, however, only said, 'You are very old, Bhaktin, and you have to work very hard; it will therefore be difficult for you to learn to read.' But Bhaktin was in no way inclined to give up the idea, and a book was given her, and the missionary's daughter gave her lessons daily in reading.

When Dharmdás heard that Bhaktin was learning to read, he was very angry. Such is the obtuseness of human nature, that it cannot for some time, even though Christian, see the good of passing the old boundaries of custom; and he was no exception to the common rule. Dharmdás, in his heart, was a very proud man. He had been the chief of the Bábá-Jí's disciples, and the people had been accustomed to defer to him, and look upon him as an oracle in religion. The Faqír, it will be remembered, appointed him priest of the Satguruwás, and chairman of the village Puncháyat. When the disciples of the Bábá-Jí were ignorant of Christianity, then he was their leader, teacher, and guide. They feared him very much, and did everything he told them to do. In all these things Dharmdás showed a great amount of spiritual pride, which we can well understand; but since Babu Hira Lall and his successor in office had taken the oversight of the Christian congregation in Phulkiya, he had not received from the Christians that deference which he thought was due to him, and which he used to receive in the past. On this account he was very angry with the brethren for not consulting him in all matters concerning their religious and moral welfare, as in the past. He saw they were no longer under his power and authority, and this angered him very much at times. He had not yet learned the lesson of humility and simplicity—to know that he should never seek authority for which he was totally unfitted by circumstances.

This will account for his asperity when Bhaktin had decided to learn to read without consulting him. If he could not command the influence of the brethren any longer, he might attempt to command her. Dharmdás called her, and asked her what profit she would get by learning to read. 'Do you wish to become our teacher?' said he. She answered mildly, and said, 'I wish to learn to read that I may for my own profit read the Word of God.' He spoke very angrily, and replied, 'You have become very independent of late. What did I say to you and the others when Premdás was married? Did I not say that no one should eat and drink with them? But you have been there, and taken your niece along with you. Do you wish to rule us all, now you are a Christian? Indeed, you are full of pride.'

Bhaktin, being very much grieved, replied very sincerely, 'Brother, what evil have I done that you are so angry with me? If the missionary was satisfied that this marriage was right and proper, why should I not go to see them? And as to the reading, I am only learning that I may be able to read the Word of God for myself. I cannot see why you are angry with me.'

On hearing this plain statement of facts, Dharmdás felt a slight twinge of conscience; he saw he was angry with her without a cause, but he did not wish to show it or appear convinced. So, rising from where he was sitting, half in anger, half in ridicule, he said, 'Very well, go on reading; we are all your humble servants.'

Bhaktin wished Tulsiya to be taught to read, but she had no desire to learn. Tulsiya was worried and troubled in mind about her husband, and so were her father, her mother, and aunt. The latter did not forget to bring her cares and sorrows to the throne of grace. She prayed the Lord to lead him to the fold of Christ, but up to the present time he showed no signs of becoming a Christian; and, with the exception of Bhaktin, all the family had lost all hope of his ever becoming a Christian.

One day Bhaktin was talking with the missionary's daughter about their prayers remaining unanswered on this particular subject. 'Before I became a Christian,' she said, 'my prayers were quickly answered, but now I am a Christian I have learned that it is necessary to leave all in the hands of God, and submit to His will. Since then some of my prayers have remained unanswered. Yes, it is quite true that we should in all things submit to His holy will, but I have been wondering what Tulsiya will do if her husband does not become a Christian. I am praying for him, and shall continue to pray till the Lord makes some arrangement for this dear child.'

The missionary's daughter replied, 'You are doing the proper thing. The Lord will surely answer your prayer, and make such arrangements for Tulsiya as will be for her good.'

Bhaktin applied herself to the task of learning to read. Whenever she had a spare moment she would either go to the missionary's daughter or to Mohini, and sit down and go over her lesson. She was slow in picking up the letters, but after much perseverance she began to recognise the larger characters; but the smaller letters she seemed to stumble over now and then. This caused Bhaktin and her teachers a good deal of trouble, and sometimes she would say, 'How shall I learn all this?'

The missionary was somewhat doubtful of her success, and took the trouble to examine her one day. She could read the larger characters distinctly, but the smaller ones she could not make out properly. The idea all at once struck him that there must be some reason for her not being able to make out the smaller characters, and he said to her, 'Perhaps your sight is growing dim, Bhaktin, therefore you cannot see the smaller letters. Take my spectacles, and see if you can manage better with them.'

But out of shyness she would not put them on, but said, 'No, sir, I can see very well; but somehow I cannot make out these small letters.'

The missionary pressed her to try the spectacles, for he was sure it was her failing sight that was at fault. After some persuasion she was prevailed upon to try the glasses. She took them up, but did not know how to put them on; sometimes the end of the frame would poke into her ear, sometimes into her hair, and in nervousness she trembled from head to foot.

The missionary's daughter took the glasses and placed them in their proper place. They were scarcely suited to Bhaktin's sight. As she put them on, a cloud came over them, and tears streamed from her eyes. She was told to keep them on and be patient. After a short time the dimness passed away, and she exclaimed in great delight, 'What big letters! These are as large as the others. Listen, I will read to you.'

In real happiness she began to laugh, and the missionary and his daughter were glad they had solved the difficulty. A pair of spectacles were at once procured, and she learned to read.

CHAPTER XVIII.

TULSIYA'S HUSBAND VISITS PHULKIYA.

THE time had now arrived, in the providence of God, when Tulsiya's prayer and the prayers of her relatives were about to be answered. The Lord was going to give them their hearts' desire, and show them He is a God who hears and answers prayer. Nothing is difficult with God. Whatever He wills, He brings about in His own way. The hearts of all men are in His hands. Like the rivers in the jungle, He can turn them as He will to accomplish His purposes.

One evening in the hot season, when Tulsiya's people had finished their daily work and taken their evening meal, they were all sitting in the verandah smoking and talking together. None of them anticipated that their prayers were now going to be answered. When the evening prayer was ended, all was perfectly still; not a sound was heard. As a rule, they were generally asleep by this time, but somehow none of them could sleep on this occasion. A gentle breeze was blowing outside, and in the house it was very warm, so they all sat down in the courtyard to enjoy the evening breeze. The clouds above passed one after another, and now and then the moon peeped out from behind the clouds, and then hid her face again, and darkness followed.

As they were sitting thus enjoying the cool air, all at once a regular thud was heard, as if some one was passing the courtyard. Tulsiya's father called and asked who was there, but no answer was returned. At last he thought he must have made some mistake; but after a short time he heard something behind the house, as if some one was standing there. The idea struck him that perhaps a thief was secretly prowling about, and he called aloud again, but there was no answer. Meanwhile the moon peeped out again from behind the clouds, and by its light he could see a man standing opposite the courtyard. He rose quickly, and, taking a large stick with him as a protection, rushed towards the man. The women of the house clung to one another for protection, trembling, and fearing they were about to be attacked and robbed of the little they had. Tulsiya's father, having reached the extremity of the courtyard, cried out, 'Who are you, and what do you want?' The man gave no answer. He then went near the man, and said, 'Speak out; what do you want?'

The strange visitor, standing outside, at length answered in a low voice, very nervously, 'I am Tulsiya's husband.'

Although he only repeated the name in a low voice, still all in the house heard him. Their fear was turned into joy, and all save Tulsiya came out to see him; she hid herself in the house. Tulsiya's father, being very much astonished, said to the young man 'Are you indeed my son-in-law? Why have you come?'

'I have come,' was the reply, 'to live with you, and join my wife.'

'Are you prepared to give up caste?' the father-in-law said.

His reply was clear and lucid. 'I should not have come to live with you if I had not been prepared to give up caste. I have run away from home for this purpose.'

They were delighted to receive him, and brought him into the house with great joy, and made him sit down and relate to them how it had all come about. All save Tulsiya gathered round him, and asked many questions, and said, 'How did you run away? What will your father say?'

The Christians living near heard their talk and expressions of joy, and came at once to see what had taken place; and, having heard the whole story, they wished Tulsiya's father and mother much joy in the return of their son-in-law. 'You see,' they said, 'the Lord has answered your prayer, and has brought this young man to you of his own free will. Indeed, those who trust in the Lord shall never be confounded.'

Undoubtedly the appearance of Tulsiya's husband was a great cause for rejoicing; but her father was very much exercised in mind about the whole affair. He was doubtful as to what his father would say on finding that his son had run away. Last time, when he paid them a visit to carry away Tulsiya, on leaving the house unsuccessful, he had said, 'I shall never set foot in this house again,' and having cursed Tulsiya and her parents, he departed in a fearful rage. If he was so angry about Tulsiya, what would he do when he found that his beloved son had left him, and run away to join his wife's people?

Tulsiya's father, on calling to mind past experience, was very much afraid, and said to his son-in-law, 'What will your father say?' His only reply was, 'I shall remain here, and shall not return to my father's house. Give me something to eat, and break my caste, and then he will be unable to take me away.'

They forthwith gave him food and water; but they were in great fear what would follow. Although it was now midnight, they sent for the catechist, and told him the whole story. 'Pray for us,' they said, 'that the Lord may have mercy upon us, and protect us from the rage of this young man's father; also that the Lord may give strength to Tulsiya's husband to remain firm in his resolve, and not to return home when his father comes to fetch him.'

They all knelt down, and the catechist prayed for Tulsiya's husband and his father; and having committed them to the care of the Lord and comforted them, he returned to his house. None of them slept that night; they were too excited, and afraid to do so. They counted the hours till morning dawned. The remaining part of the night seemed an age, and, their hearts being full of fear, they said one to another, 'When his father finds out that his son has run away and come here, what will he say? what will he do? Who knows?'

Bhaktin advised her brother and his wife to put their trust in the Lord, and showed them how He had answered their prayers, and brought their son-in-law to Phulkiya. 'Do you think he will run off again? God will never permit that.'

In the morning a Christian came running, and brought the news that Tulsiya's father-in-law was coming to the village, and bringing a half-a-dozen men with him The whole family was in fear and trembling; they dreaded the result of this visit. The little children ran and hid themselves in the house, yea, even the house-dogs barked and showed their teeth, and seemed to understand that something remarkable was about to take place. The young husband and Tulsiya's father stood before the courtyard, greatly troubled and perplexed, watching the approach of the invaders. Each one was in great fear lest Tulsiya's father-in-law should vent his spleen upon him.

CHAPTER XIX.

THE MEETING OF FATHER AND SON.

AFTER a short time, the old father, supporting himself on his stick, bent with the burden of grief, came slowly forward and sat down in one corner of the verandah of the house; and those who were with him followed his example, and seated themselves in the verandah. None of them made his salutation, and none of the people of the house saluted them. The old man did not show any anger, but was bent down with grief and sorrow. He put his head between his knees, and began to weep most piteously.

His son, in order to bear up against the anger of his father, had steeled himself to face him; but when he saw him in great grief, and heard his cry of sorrow, his heart was touched, and he sat down and began to cry also. The women and children, out of sympathy with their sorrow, mingled their tears with the rest. All this took place, as it were, in a moment; none had anticipated it. They were prepared for fearful results, and were expecting a dreadful quarrel; but none of them thought the old man would be so filled with grief that anger would find no place in his heart.

The old man, weeping, thus opened the conversation with his son: 'Oh, my son, why have you done this? Why have you forsaken your old father? Come, my son, let us go home. Your mother is weeping at home, and beating her breasts and her head against the floor in sorrow, as if she would lose her senses.'

Having thus bemoaned his lot, he began to cry and sob as if his heart would break. He then again described his sad lot and that of his poor wife in such pitiable terms, that the heart of his son was touched, and he began to weep louder than before. His father then besought him to come and sit near him. But he, sobbing, replied, 'I cannot.' The father asked, 'Why not, my son?' But his son did not answer for a minute or two. Then, in a trembling voice, quite abashed, he gave answer, 'I cannot, because I have broken my caste.'

There was a terrible struggle going on in the father's heart as he thought over these words and all they meant to him; they were like a death-knell to him. For two or three minutes his countenance was like adamant, and he could not speak. Affection struggled against anger and wrath, and it was difficult to calculate which would conquer. At last he hoarsely cried out, 'Never mind; it does not matter. I will pay a fine to the Brahmins to restore you to caste. My son, come along with me.' Having said this, he rose and turned towards his son; but the young man placed his back against the wall, and said decidedly, 'I cannot go with you.'

His father tried in every way to persuade and influence him; but it was of no use, he remained firm in his decision. Upon this the young man's uncle, who had come with his father, got very angry, and began to use abusive language, curse, and reproach him. Gradually his father joined in these fearful reproaches, and his anger lost all bounds. At last he poured upon his head all the curses and reproaches he had previously bestowed on Tulsiya and her parents.

They thought by this treatment to frighten Tulsiya's husband, but they miserably failed in their object. When his son heard all these fearful imprecations and curses, he steeled his heart, and finally decided that he would not on any consideration return with his father. When his uncle saw that all their endeavours were in vain, and that his nephew was not at all afraid, he said to his brother, 'Let us leave this house and all its cursed brood, for the people in it are of the meanest and lowest caste.'

Tulsiya's father-in-law rose in a dreadful rage, and, having delivered himself of two or three more cutting sentences, full of imprecations, he followed his friends and left the house. Tulsiya and her relatives now began to breathe freely, for they felt the crisis had passed. They wondered greatly how it came about that this fickle young man had all at once shown the spirit of bravery and become strong—so strong that even his father's supplications and tears went unheeded, and his anger unregarded. He received courage to refuse to leave his wife. This was indeed a wonder to them all.

They were convinced he had not endured all this for Christ's sake, for the love of Christ was not in his heart; and they also knew it could not altogether be the result of affection for Tulsiya, for he loved his father and mother more than any one else—he was their petted and spoiled child. When they were talking over this interview between father and son amongst themselves, Tulsiya's husband confessed he could not tell why he was unwilling to proceed with his father. 'When he wept so loudly,' he added, 'I said in my heart I must return with him, but something forbade me doing so, and therefore I refused.'

'My son,' said dear old Bhaktin, having smothered her tears, 'our prayers to the Lord of Hosts had so bound you that you were unable to go; this is my opinion.'

After this event, Tulsiya's husband lived in peace in his father-in-law's house. His wife's family were so overjoyed at his coming that they pampered his tastes and waited on him at every turn; whatever he desired in the way of food they prepared for him. He was petted and pampered more in his father-in-law's house than he had been at home—a sure way to spoil the energies of any young man.

Gradually the harvest-time came, and there was much work to be done. His father-in-law told him to go into the fields and work. Such a command was not agreeable to the tastes of this young man, and when pressure was brought to bear upon him he went off in a fit of anger, and returned to his father's village.

Tulsiya's family were very much alarmed at this turn of affairs, for they were doubtful about the results of it all. Their grief was so great that for two or three days no regular food was cooked in the house.

But Tulsiya's husband was very much undeceived on reaching home. His father would not allow him to enter the house, and in a severe and snarling tone turned on him fiercely, and said, 'Who are you? My son is dead and forgotten; I have mourned and lamented his death, and have at last washed my hands of him; who are you, then? Go away out of this house.' His mother, on seeing her son, longed to clasp him to her breast, but she could only weep and lament; she was helpless. Insomuch as he had eaten and drunk with the Christians, his parents could not receive him into their house. His mother advised her son to go to the Brahmins and explain everything, and arrange with them for restoration to caste.

The young man acted on his mother's advice; but the Brahmins, for reasons of their own, demanded such a large sum that it would have been impossible for his parents to pay it. He besought the Brahmins with folded hands to reduce the fine. At first they would not consent; but at last, after much haggling on both sides, they said, 'Very well; bring your wife, and then we will see what can be done.'

Tulsiya's husband knew very well that she would not agree to such terms, and leave her father and mother and give up Christianity; therefore, losing all heart, he went about here and there for two or three days, not knowing what to do. From a sense of shame he did not like to return to his father-in-law's house, but there was no other place where he could go.

At last, having humbled his proud heart, he returned to Phulkiya and joined his wife's family, and began to work a little for his bread. But he was very lazy, and his father-in-law was much troubled about him. All tried to explain to him that God had made the man to be the bread-winner, and it was not proper and fit of him to sit lazy at home; but he would listen to no one.

One day it happened that he was ordered to go in the field and plough. He shrank away, refused, and went and lay down on his bed in the house. When he would listen to no persuasions, Bhaktin went and sat near the bed, and, weeping, said, 'Oh, my son, my son, why do you act in this way? Why do you trouble us so much? See, my son, you did not wish to flee from the service of Satan; you did not consider for a moment how you were to escape the torments of hell; but I prayed day and night that you might become a Christian, and God heard my prayers, which, with strong crying and tears, I made before Him, and brought you here. And now you act in this way! My son, do come to your senses!'

Tulsiya's husband was much ashamed of himself after this plain and touching entreaty, and could return no answer. He rose from the bed without uttering a word, and went quietly to his work. From that day he began to amend; and when he would listen to no one else Bhaktin would use her persuasive powers, and, hanging down his head, he would do as he was bid.

CHAPTER XX.

THE POWER OF CHRISTIAN LOVE.

WHEN the hot weather was drawing to a close, and the people began to prepare for the rains, an unexpected difficulty presented itself to the Christians of Phulkiya. There was a boat belonging to the village; it was of great use to the cultivators during this season of the year. The people carried their produce to the market at Sáhibganj on the boat during the rains, as there was no other means of reaching the higher tableland beyond the influence of the flood. In it they also conveyed their cattle from the village. Whilst the water was low, the animals could wade through the water, but when it came in all its force from the river their village became an island, or like a number of small islands, for the water found its way on the roads, and reached their very doors.

From the day that Premdás' marriage took place, the people of the village began again to trouble the Christians very much; and when the rains were about to break, the Hindus said to the Christians, 'Whatever befalls you during this season, we have made up our minds that none of the Christians shall use our boat. Make your own arrangements, and do not expect the use of our boat.'

The Christians besought them very earnestly not to do them this injustice. 'What shall we do?' they said; 'and how shall we and our cattle manage to live through the rains if you treat us in this way? We are willing to pay you for the use of the boat, and have no wish to use it without paying you for it.'

But the Hindus would not agree to any arrangement, and held them in fear and terror by the threat. In their fear and helplessness, the Christians promised to pay double the amount of any one else, if they would only permit them to use the boat; but the Hindus were inflexible.

Fear, terror, and death stared the Christians in the face, for they saw no way out of the difficulty. At last they sent a deputation, consisting of the catechist, Dharmdás, and several others, to acquaint the missionary with their difficulty, and ask his advice. When he heard the whole story, he told them they must have a boat of their own. But they at once replied, 'How is it possible for us to find the money for such an expensive article?'

The missionary advised them to make a collection in every family, as much as each could give, and also to seek help from the Christians in Bhágalpur. 'You will be able,' he said, 'to see how much you can collect; and after you have done that, come and inform me of the result, and I will advise you further.'

They at once opened a subscription list, and when the amount collected in Phulkiya was added to that given in Bhágalpur, they found they had not half the amount required for the boat. They said, however, among them-

selves, 'We have a Helper in heaven. Our Heavenly Father will at all times show His people a way out of their difficulties.'

In Bhágalpur there was a godly and kind colonel, attached to the regiment stationed there. He showed great affection for the Christians, and sometimes went to worship in their church. He and his good wife gave considerable help to the Institution for Orphan Boys and Girls. Their purse was ever open for the use of the Mission. And we are sure the blessing of the Lord will follow them for remembering His people! They were always trying to help others to be happy.

As an instance of kind thoughtfulness, we give the following:—On one occasion they went for a drive some distance in the country, and near a tank they saw some large beautiful shells. The colonel ordered his coachman to collect a large number, and put them in the carriage. On reaching home, he had them cleaned, and afterwards took them and divided them with his own hands amongst the orphan children, saying, 'I know children like these things very much.'

Another day the colonel shot an alligator, and ordered it to be put on a bullock-cart, and shown to the orphans, saying, 'Possibly they have never seen such an animal.' Another day the boys of the Orphanage were flying kites for amusement. The string broke, and the kite went on the parade ground, where the colonel was going to drill his troops. He guessed it had come from the Orphanage, and ordered one of the men to bring it to him. At his leisure he took it to the Mission, and gave it back to the children. On Christmas day the colonel and his good wife made a feast for the orphan children and their teachers, and fed them with sweetmeats, Christmas cake, and tea. They also distributed to the children toys from

Calcutta, and altogether made it a very pleasant and happy day for the children.

When the colonel heard of the difficulties which beset the disciples of the Bábá-Jí, he called the deputation to his house, and asked them how much they had collected, and how much more they required to enable them to purchase the boat. When they had told him, he replied, 'Very well, my dear friends; I will give you the balance, nay, even more than that; so go and buy yourselves a good strong boat.' When they heard him make this generous offer, they thanked him most heartily, and said, 'Your kindness has saved our cattle. We were drowning, and you put out a helping hand to save us. May the Lord bless you and your children!'

These new disciples of Jesus returned to Phulkiya blessing and praising the Lord Jesus, and on their way they bought a boat at Sáhibganj.

This year the rains broke earlier than usual, and the floods came on sooner than usual. Phulkiya and the villages around it were flooded in a couple of days. The Indian corn had not yet been cut, for it was still unripe. The cultivators sustained great losses by this early rush of the flood. They began to cut the Indian corn with the water up to their waist, in order to feed the animals on it. Their cattle were still in the village, and had not yet been taken to the higher ground for protection. Some of the cultivators, in their haste, turned their cattle into the water, that they might swim to the shore; but some of them were carried away by the flood, and others were drowned, and the cattle and goats that remained in the village began to suffer from the surrounding flood, and get ill.

In their new boat the Christians carried their cattle, grass, straw, etc., to the higher land with great facility, and sat comfortably in their shelter. Now the time came for the Hindus in the village to fall into difficulties and seek help from the Christians. They came most humbly to the Christians, and said, 'We did indeed commit a great sin in refusing to allow you the use of our boat; it was wrong of us to quarrel with you about it. Forgive us, and do not remember our misdeeds, but let us have your boat to send our cattle away; and whatever you charge for the use of it we shall be glad to give, because our animals are perishing in the village.'

Had the Christians desired to show now the spirit of revenge for their past conduct, it would not have been at all surprising, though it would have been unchristian; but God saved them from an uncharitable spirit, and gave them a merciful mind. They consulted the catechist, and called the villagers, and said, 'You can use our boat, but we cannot possibly take anything for the use of it. God gave us this boat, and helped us out of our difficulties, otherwise we should have been drowned. Take the boat and use it, and bless the name of the Lord, who gave it to us for the hour of difficulty.'

When the Hindus of the village experienced this act of pure and simple love, their hearts were very much softened, and with great humility they said, 'From henceforth we shall trouble you no more about your religion, nor shall we place any difficulties in your way. Whatever has taken place is forgotten and forgiven. Go on serving the Lord Jesus. It is true that none but Christians would show such love and affection to their enemies.'

From this time the people of the village began to return the affection of the Christians, and they called the Christian boat 'The Boat of Love.' Dharmdás said to the catechist, on seeing the good result from their loving example, 'You gave us good advice, and the saying is true that the boat of love can rise above the highest mountains. See how love has risen above years of hatred and enmity from the affection and hearts of these people. And if we allowed them to use the boat free, what does it matter? We got this boat to help us in our difficulty, and see how the mercy of God has been manifested in it all!'

CHAPTER XXI.

THE TRIUMPH OF FAITH.

BHAKTIN was very anxious that Tulsiya's husband should be baptized, and the catechist was instructing him for this purpose. When the cold season came round again, and the missionary came to Phulkiya, Bhaktin took Tulsiya's husband to see him. He examined him, and was satisfied with his answers, and promised to baptize him. But it is difficult to understand what spirit possessed Tulsiya's husband, and what was in his heart; in a fractious and independent manner he informed the missionary that when he was baptized he would require a sum of money from him. With this money he had made up his mind to build a house, and separate himself from his father-in-law. 'I shall have my own house,' he said; 'so please instruct my father-in-law to give me my share in his estate.'

Up to this time this young man had never divulged the inner workings of his mind, and when Bhaktin heard him make such an astounding demand she was perfectly confounded, and became as one dumb. But the missionary said, 'My son, I shall not give you money, nor baptize you; I see you do not understand the meaning of baptism. You must come to me every day for half-an-hour, and I will instruct you in the Christian religion; then, my son, by God's grace, your eyes may be opened, and you may understand what kind of people are baptized, and with what motives.'

The missionary then asked him who gave him this idea of asking for money when he was baptized. He answered, 'Some one told me to demand a sum of money, and I should get it. The Brahmins say that the Government gives you lots of money each time a man is made a Christian, and this is the reason you travel so far to make converts, and have come to Phulkiya to make us Christians.'

Bhaktin was very much alarmed at his impertinence, and desired to get him away somehow, and take him home. But the missionary saw her confusion, and said, 'Sit still, Bhaktin; it does not matter; do not trouble yourself. Listen to me, both of you. Yesterday the headman of Mahaganj village came to visit me, and he was very solicitous to know how many rupees the Government gave me for making a native a Christian. What, for instance, would they give if I made him a Christian? "Some say," he added, "that for every Christian you make the Government gives you one hundred rupees, others say you get fifty, but I wish now to know the real truth of the matter." It was with the greatest difficulty I could make him understand that I was neither a Government servant nor in any way connected with Government. I told him that Government does not give a farthing to missionaries for making native Christians; that I am a preacher of the Gospel of our Lord Jesus Christ, according to His command; and my necessary expenses are paid by the religious people of

England, and all the money is collected in voluntary subscriptions.'

Bhaktin replied with great deference, 'How can the heathen know all this? They talk all kinds of nonsense on this subject.'

From that day Tulsiya's husband received daily instruction. He several times begged to be baptized, and said, 'I only wish for baptism; please forgive all my ignorance and impertinence.'

But the missionary replied, 'No, my son; we cannot do things so quickly as that. We must now see, from your life and conduct, that you are making a man of yourself. You have done very little up to the present time to earn your own living; sometimes you have worked a little, but have often been sitting idle at home. Give up your lazy habits, and work for your father-in-law faithfully like a true son, then I shall be convinced you wish to be a true Christian.'

The missionary did not baptize Tulsiya's husband that cold season; but during the hot season duty called him to Phulkiya, and the father-in-law begged that his son-in-law's desire for baptism should now be regarded. He gave a very good account of him, and stated that he had become more humble and docile, and had given his mind fairly to work. There being no further objections, the missionary baptized him in the presence of Premdás, his wife's people, and the brethren.

In this way the disciples of the Bábá-Jí, after having passed through many trials and sorrows, had at last become Christians. Many of them were true and simple-minded disciples of Jesus. Some of them, through fear of dying a dreadful death in unbelief, had become Christians, and a few from worldly motives had cast in their lot with the servants of the Lord Jesus; but, though they were all called Christians, still some of them retained a leaven of their old religion, worldly customs, and ways. There were still instances amongst them of brethren who found it difficult all at once to cast off their belief in sorcery and their fear of their old deities. And of those who were true Christians, some were babes in Christ, their faith was weak, and there were faults in their character; but as this new congregation advanced in the knowledge of our Lord and Saviour Jesus Christ, they gradually improved, and desired to grow in grace, faith, and power. They prayed to the Holy Spirit to water the seed of faith sown in their hearts, and to make them flower and bear fruit, and show they were a chosen race to magnify the name of God. Sometimes they would sing this song in their own native tongue:

> 'Come, gracious Lord, our prayers do Thou hear!
> We are children, Thy household, teach us Thy fear;
> Give us experience, and make us all wise;
> Water Thy small plant, that heaven we may prize;
> Make us all fruitful, and give us Thy grace,
> That we all may at length see Thy dear face.'

The first fruit which ripened for the Lord's kingdom in Phulkiya was Jethú the leper. He gradually became weaker and weaker and more helpless; but his wife and family did not realise the approach of death, because he had been ill for so long. One night he fell asleep, and never woke again; he was called home, and went to that world where pain is unknown, and sorrow and sighing flee away.

After Jethú, the Lord called Bhaktin. She had gone on growing in grace, and her life was one lesson of humility to all; she had ripened quickly for that heavenly kingdom. One day she said to her Christian sisters, 'Do not call me Bhaktin the saint, but Papin the sinner. Call me, if you like, " beloved ; " for the Lord hath loved me, and given Himself for me.' After the baptism of Tulsiya's husband, at the end of the rains, she was taken ill, and did not recover. As she grew weaker each day, she seemed to have a presentiment that her hour was come; but she had no fear, for 'she knew in whom she had believed, and was assured that He was able to save to the uttermost them that come unto God by Him,' and she longed to enter into the Master's presence.

During her sickness the Christian and Hindu women of the village used to visit her and sit by her, to try and comfort her; but, after all, Bhaktin was the real comforter. One day, when the mother of the young lad who had been raised up by Bhaktin's prayers came to see her, she in conversation said to her, 'Dear sister, have you no fear at all ? Do you know where you are going ?'

Bhaktin replied, 'Why should I be afraid ? I am going to Him whose servant I am. He is my hope and trust. He will bring me safely through the deep waters. He is the same who delivered your son from the jaws of death, and gave him to you again.'

The woman answered, with tears in her eyes, 'I do believe in Him; but my husband hates to hear His precious name. When I try to pray to Him and sing His praises in Christian songs, he threatens to beat me.'

Bhaktin replied, 'Do not give up. Go on, and acknowledge the Lord Jesus in your heart, and pray daily for your husband. God can soften his heart.'

One day Bhaktin called Dharmdás, and said, 'Brother, I feel my time is now short. I want you to forgive me. Once or twice I have said things to grieve you, but forget it all, and forgive me.'

Dharmdás replied, with great affection, 'Dearest sister

it is necessary for you to forgive me, and not for me to forgive you. You never wronged me, or spoke unadvisedly; but I was very obstinate and proud. May the Lord forgive me! And do you, dear sister, forgive me also.'

Bhaktin's face lighted up with divine happiness, and she said to Tulsiya, who waited on her day and night, 'Listen, my daughter: when I was a disciple of the Bábá-Jí, I looked upon Dharmdás as my spiritual guide; do you look up to him also, and honour him in the Lord.'

Dharmdás' eyes filled with tears, and he said in a low voice, as if speaking to himself, 'How good and loving she is! Oh, how little of her spirit do I feel!'

When Bhaktin was called away, the Christians buried her near the graves of Jethú and Babu Hira Lall.

Many of the Lord's people from Phulkiya now sleep in hope; and when the Lord Jesus comes again to receive His beloved ones, many from this village will be caught up to meet their Lord in the air, and so shall they be ever with the Lord. They shall receive the reward of faith, even eternal happiness and peace in the mansions above.

PREFATORY NOTE

THE Rev. Tulsi Paul, first pastor of the Native Christian colony of Annfield, Dehra Doon, North India, was a convert from Hinduism. About twenty years after his baptism, and only three years before his death, he wrote, at the express wish of a missionary, the narrative of his life From childhood to the time of his baptism. This autobiography gives vivid and graphic touches of the spiritual struggles and conflicts of a mind steeped in Hinduism, before truth could conquer and he was enabled to say, 'The conclusion of it all was, that at last our Lord Jesus Christ was victorious, and I accepted baptism.'

The sketch is written in a true Oriental style. The history of his life is interwoven with proverbs, lines of Persian and Hindi poetry, rhymed sentences, and with long poetical compositions of his own.

A translation of the pamphlet exactly as it was written would prove tedious, and hence only extracts from it have been taken for the memoir. The facts and incidents relating to him after his baptism have been kindly supplied by Mrs. Lamb, widow of the late Rev. I. Lamb, missionary of Meerut; and by Mrs. Guichet, daughter of Major Rind; and by the Rev. W. Baumann, missionary of Fyzabad, who has also added the contents of the last chapter, having been with the Rev. Tulsi Paul during his last years.

it is necessary for you to forgive me, and not for n
to forgive you. You never wronged me, or spoke u
advisedly; but I was very obstinate and proud. M[r]
the Lord forgive me! And do you, dear sister, forgiv
me also.'

Bhaktin's face lighted up with divine happiness, and
she said to Tulsiya, who waited on her day and night,
'Listen, my daughter: when I was a disciple of the Bábá-
Jí, I looked upon Dharmdás as my spiritual guide; d
you look up to him also, and honour him in the Lord.'

Dharmdás' eyes filled with tears, and he said in a lo
voice, as if speaking to himself, 'How good and lovi[ng]
she is! Oh, how little of her spirit do I feel!'

When Bhaktin was called away, the Christians burie[d]
her near the graves of Jethú and Babu Hira Lall.

Many of the Lord's people from Phulkiya now sle[ep]
in hope; and when the Lord Jesus comes again to recei[ve]
His beloved ones, many from this village will be caug[ht]
up to meet their Lord in the air, and so shall they
ever with the Lord. They shall receive the reward
faith, even eternal happiness and peace in the mansio[ns]
above.

PREFATORY NOTE

THE Rev. Tulsi Paul, first pastor of the Native Christian colony of Annfield, Dehra Doon, North India, was a convert from Hinduism. About twenty years after his baptism, and only three years before his death, he wrote, at the express wish of a missionary, the narrative of his life from childhood to the time of his baptism. This autobiography gives vivid and graphic touches of the spiritual struggles and conflicts of a mind steeped in Hinduism, before truth could conquer and he was enabled to say, 'The conclusion of it all was, that at last our Lord Jesus Christ was victorious, and I accepted baptism.'

The sketch is written in a true Oriental style. The history of his life is interwoven with proverbs, lines of Persian and Hindi poetry, rhymed sentences, and with long poetical compositions of his own.

A translation of the pamphlet exactly as it was written would prove tedious, and hence only extracts from it have been taken for the memoir. The facts and incidents relating to him after his baptism have been kindly supplied by Mrs. Lamb, widow of the late Rev. M. Lamb, missionary of Meerut; and by Mrs. Guichet, daughter of Major Rind; and by the Rev. W. Baumann, missionary of Fyzabad, who has also added the contents of the last chapter, having been with the Rev. Tulsi Paul during his last years.

CHAPTER I.

TULSI PAUL'S WEDDING AND HIS STUDIES.

TULSI[1] PAUL[2] was the younger son of the landowner, Mansa Ram, of Koelra, in Oude, India. His father belonged to the Kayasth caste, who generally are clerks and copyists, and Mansa Ram was the head clerk of the estate of the Rajah Nawal Singh, of Bulrampore.

Tulsi Paul writes in his autobiography: 'I am beginning my history from the time when my reasoning powers awoke, and I commenced to think and to ponder, and to understand matters, and the first thing I remember in my life was my wedding.' This took place, according to Hindu custom, when he was a mere child. Writing about it, he says: 'At the appointed time a Brahmin and a barber[3] brought the *tilak*[4] to our house. Then our house-priest began to observe the stars, in order to find out a propitious and lucky day for commencing

---

[1] The Hindi name of the plant *Ocimum sanctum*, worshipped by the Hindus.

[2] He received the name of Paul at his baptism. His heathen name was Tulsi Ram.

[3] The barbers act as go-betweens in marriage affairs.

[4] Nuptial gifts sent from the bride's house to the bridegroom.

the wedding ceremonies, which was done by putting the *tikā* on my forehead. When the lucky day had been ascertained, there was great rejoicing in our house. My mother was especially happy at the thought of her son's wedding, and all my friends and relatives assembled for the festive occasion. Every one greeted me, and praised me, saying, "You are a lucky fellow; now go in, and win the prize."

'I was set on a *vedi* [throne or platform], and, in the presence of my parents and all my relatives, and the Brahmins, was bathed and dressed in state, the women in the meanwhile singing songs. The beating of drums and other music was kept up the whole day. A number of Brahmins and astronomers were sitting here and there, chanting and making prayers, and reading in their books, in order to find out my fate, and accepted the money which every one in the house was laying down before them, in hopes that they would find out a lucky fate for me; but none of them discovered my real destiny! [Tulsi Paul here evidently refers to his becoming a Christian.]

'Then they prepared the *tikā*. Some *haldi* [turmeric] was ground to powder, and my forehead marked with it, and then some whole grains of rice were stuck on.[1] After this ceremony I was ordered by my mother to make obeisance to all in the house. The women in the meantime were singing marriage songs, and joking and playing with me and with each other, and many heathen customs and rites were gone through. Then they took me from the platform to another place, where the wedding guests had to present to me their gold mohurs,[2] and where a brass platter, with rice and *haldi*, and other eatables put

---

[1] Rice being the symbol of food, and *haldi* of spices, viz. abundance.

[2] A kind of fee each guest is expected to pay towards the expenses of the wedding.

up in leaves, were set down before me. All the time I was being teased and praised and flattered. They called me the sun, and the bride the moon, and that I was indeed a beautiful bridegroom. I did not say anything, but I was thinking deeply, and observing all I saw and heard, and my heart was rent with shyness and confusion.

'My mother now led me to an inner room to make my obeisance to our house-gods, and to perform worship before them. She made me also worship my ancestors, and stone, earth, and water. I went as submissively as a monkey led by his keeper, for I was as helpless as a bird entrapped in a net. I was but a child, and altogether in the power of my mother, who made me do what she thought right. Oh, my heart yearns over my poor simple-minded mother, who is altogether under the influence of Brahmins and priests! As to my father, he too was a zealous idol-worshipper.

'My whole wedding was to me like a play in which I was the chief actor. I enjoyed the fun of the many ceremonies I had to go through, and the being made so much of; but I little guessed how I was being drawn into a net from which there would be no escape all the rest of my life. Ah! those around me were making merry music, drumming and piping for joy and gladness, while a chain of sorrow was being riveted round my neck! [His wife outlived him, and remained to the last a strict Hindu.] The ceremonies I went through made a deep impression on me. It was like being crowned king. While I was bathed, the women sang marriage songs. I was dressed up in the customary white and yellow wedding garments. A yellow turban with gold border was put on my head. My aunt painted my eyes with lamp-black, and ear-rings were put into my ears. When I was ready I was put on a throne, and all praised and complimented me on my appearance.

'My elder brother borrowed a beautiful palanquin from the rajah. They put me in, and had me carried about, whilst money was distributed among the Brahmins, and thrown amongst the crowd. Then a procession was formed, and I was carried to Gonda, the town where the bride lived. We arrived there at night, accompanied with the music of flutes, trumpets, horns, and drums. The men were carrying torches, and the dancing-girls performing as they went along. The bride's procession came out to meet us, and both processions united. It was indeed an imposing sight, for about a thousand people were collected, and all were singing and shouting and flattering the bridegroom, and counting the bride very lucky that fate had apportioned to her such a beautiful bridegroom.

'I, of course, enjoyed all this gay scene, because in those days I had not yet learned to care for God; but still I was not happy or at ease. I was all along thinking of the examination which, according to the custom of our caste, was awaiting me at the bride's house. When the procession arrived there, I managed with great difficulty to enter the courtyard. [The bridegroom is beaten with sticks and brooms made of paper flowers, and prevented entering till he has paid a handsome bribe.] There I found myself in the presence of crowds of women, who drew me into their midst, and began my dreaded examination by saying, "Now, little one, rehearse something—a song or a proverb, and show that you have learned something, and then enter the house."[1]

---

[1] Among the Kayasths, the bridegroom gets a present according to the amount of knowledge he possesses, and naturally would feel ashamed at receiving only a small sum, if he does not satisfy his bride's relatives.

'Well, I quoted, among other things, some stanzas which I had been taught to say, viz.:

> '"I have performed all the marriage ceremonies,
> And what do I get for all my pains?
> Nothing but a worthless woman."'

After Tulsi Paul's wedding he was set to his studies, and, being of the Kayasth caste, his chief accomplishment consisted in writing a good hand; and so beautifully could he write the native characters, that it was said he could write like print with his eyes shut. But he was also very fond of his books, and anxious to acquire all the knowledge his old orthodox teachers were able to impart. People used to say he had gone mad after his books, and he was so well read in Hindu religious literature that Bishop French once remarked he wished he could quote Scripture as easily as Tulsi Paul did his Hindu Shastras.

Tulsi Paul writes about his studies:—

'After reading the Hindus' books, I took up those of the Mohammedans, and at last also studied the Koran, which the Mohammedans call divine; but nowhere did I find truth. I only found the different religious guides fighting about the truth, contradicting each other, and each thinking he possessed the truth. Wherever I heard of a famous teacher or of a good school, I left home, and went there in search of more knowledge. I felt dissatisfied, and as if something was wanting which I wished to attain to. There was a yearning in my heart to get to know the truth, and to find God; and I thought that through much study I should attain my desire. So I strove on, minding neither hunger nor thirst, cold nor heat, nor any other privation. For months at a time I cooked only one meal a day; and as I did not know how to make bread [fresh unleavened thin cakes], I made balls of wheat and water, and boiled these, and ate them with the cheapest pulse. My whole being was wrapped up in the service of my teachers and religious guides. I waited on them day and night, and cared for nothing but to advance in knowledge and learning. But, alas! what kind of religious guides and instructors were ours? They did not even allow their disciples to ask questions; they were simply to believe all they told them. We were taught to pay them divine homage, and follow them implicitly, yet not to mind their personal example, for they had attained such a degree of holiness that they had the power and the liberty to do as they pleased.

'Both the priests and the religious guides who wished us to pay them divine honour, and their gods whom they taught us to worship, were frivolous and sinful. Should we worship the feet of the light-minded priest, or bow down before his sinning god? Ah! in those days, when I was seeking truth, I would have laid down my life for a teacher who would have been pure and holy, and had shown to me the true way of coming into God's favour.'

K

HINDU FAQIR.

CHAPTER II.

SOME PHASES OF IDOLATRY.

'IT is astonishing,' writes Tulsi Paul, 'how our religious guides and teachers coerced our wills, and brought us into subjection to themselves. They would say, for instance, "Remember the curse, 'Whosoever cheats[1] his religious guide, or robs[2] his priest, shall become poor and a leper.'"

'We stood in such dread of our guides, that, rather than run the risk of incurring their curse, we would give them all they wanted, and more. And they had many different ways and means of satisfying their greed and covetousness, by promising us present and future rewards and blessings. But oh, they are all like empty, hollow bamboos, and steeped in errors and sins, although they take so much pains to appear righteous before men, and to attain that appearance of sanctity which will bring the common run of men to their feet.

'Some, in order to appear holy, grow long beards; others shave their heads, and fulfil vows. Some rub ashes on their bodies; others, with the same object in

---

[1] By not supplying him abundantly.
[2] By refusing any of his requests.

view, walk about in red garments; and others again wear rags and tattered clothes. Some sit moping in self-imposed silence, never even lifting their heads; whilst others stalk about chanting and shouting their god's name, and blowing horns and playing on cymbals, abusing without fear or shame those who give them nothing.

'Some hang down from trees, head downward; others live under umbrellas made of leaves. Some paint the sign of their god on their foreheads, and others keep on muttering their names, day and night, over their rosaries. Many go long pilgrimages, carrying holy Ganges water, and selling it as a means of washing away sin.

'Many deck themselves with all kinds of amulets and talismans and charms. Again, many go in for sorcery, witchcraft, fortune-telling, and the reading of the destiny of man from the stars; but oh, their soothsayings fly away and disappear like the chaff of the wheat. They lie, they cheat, they set traps, they spread nets. They are the monkey-keepers, and the world is the monkey which dances according to their order!

'Among other things, my religious teacher told me I must take the *mantar*,[1] or God would be angry, and cast me into hell. There I should have to hold with both hands a burning pillar of fire, and weep and repent of my irreligiousness. I was also informed that during the transmigration of my soul it was very unlikely I should happen to be born a human being, and have the sense to secure my final salvation, so I had better take the *mantar* and be safe.'

Tulsi Paul hesitated long before taking this step. From childhood he had been taught to worship the god Ram, whose name he bore, and to trust in him. He was

---

[1] A sacred formula whispered into the ear by a religious guide, to be kept as a motto, and given only to those who intend leading a religious life.

also worshipping the *Salagram* (emblem of the god Shiew). Besides, his father had taken him in early youth to the Ganges, to have his sins washed away. He had also done many meritorious acts, such as washing the feet of Brahmins and drinking of the water, and begging them for *prashad* (a little of the food a Brahmin has cooked for himself, given as a blessing), and he did not see the necessity of making the profession of a religious life, such as taking the *mantar* presupposed. At last, however, his teacher induced him to obey; 'for,' adds Tulsi Paul,

HINDUS BATHING IN THE GANGES.

'if they commanded anything, who were we that we could resist them? We were altogether in their power, and as helpless as men who have drunk of the waters of a well drugged with opium.'

So he paid all the fees, and went through the ceremony of taking the *mantar*. The candidate, after going through various baths and purifications, presents himself before his spiritual guide. After performing various ceremonies, the latter whispers the charm repeatedly into the ear of the disciple, who during the performance has to hold out his hand, into which his priest puts some grains of raw rice, upon which he has blown, in order to consecrate it. The disciple chews these whilst listening to the chanting of the *mantar*.[1]

Of the result of taking the *mantar*, Tulsi Paul writes:

'When I mastered the charm whispered to me, pride filled my soul, and I began to look upon myself as possessing the knowledge of all mysteries, and as having become holy and perfect. I said to my spiritual guide, "O Bábá-Jí [spiritual father], impart to me yet another *mantar*, which will bring me great wealth, and a great name of sanctity. I would like people to say, 'Tulsi Ram is indeed a holy man. See how rich he is, and how bountifully he gives of his riches to the Brahmins.'" Behold, what pride was stirring in my heart!

'My guide answered me, saying, "Son, all this is contained in the charm you have received."

'Well, what could I say?'

After some time a new religious teacher appeared in the village where Tulsi Paul lived. He made a great stir with his austerity and sanctity. Tulsi Paul became his devoted disciple, and imitated him in all his religious acts and devotions, and in his asceticism, hoping thereby to attain holiness, and ingratiate himself with God.

But his health began to suffer, and his elder brother put a stop to his efforts, saying, 'Do you not know the proverb, that those who merely copy and imitate devotees in their austerities waste away and die? This sort of life is not for you; it is only for very holy persons, who feel constrained from within to do all this of themselves.'

'So I felt rebuked,' writes Tulsi Paul, 'and thought

[1] A symbol that, as rice feeds the body, the *mantar* is entering the soul.

myself unworthy to continue these practices, and desisted; yet I went on inquiring how I should find God.'

He was next advised to give himself to the worship of Maha-deo (the great god), who would give him all he asked for. But there was one restriction: he must never eat anything of the offerings presented to this god, or he would become a dog in his next birth. He was further informed that all dogs had been men in their former birth who had eaten of the offerings of this great god. Tulsi Paul set himself the task of serving and worshipping Maha-deo; but his heart did not feel satisfied, nor did he find peace. Of his doubts and perplexities he writes as follows:—

'"What!" said I to myself, "at times I am worshipping this god faithfully and loyally, and yet, if I but touch what has been offered to him, I am to be turned into a dog in my next birth!" However, I clung to him some time longer, offering daily a certain quantity of *achhat*;[1] but one day I could not succeed in getting any, and then, somehow, the whole affair seemed very unsatisfactory, and I felt grieved and sore at heart. I went off to a lonely place, and began to weep. The thought rose again and again, that it was useless to worship this god. If he could not help me to procure a little *achhat* for his own offering, he surely would not be able either to give me the great things for my soul I was asking him for.'

So Tulsi Paul forsook this god also, and, not knowing what better to do, he returned to the worship of the god of his childhood, Ram. And he found some satisfaction in getting the pundits to read and expound the Ramayan to him, and in learning portions of it by heart.

---

[1] Whole unbroken rice, used in oblations. It is husked by rubbing it between the palms of the hand instead of in a mortar. This work being laborious and troublesome, such rice is not always obtainable.

His elder brother seems to have sympathised with Tulsi Paul in his search after truth and peace, although he himself felt perfectly satisfied with his own form of worship. Tulsi Paul says of him: 'My elder brother remained a loyal worshipper of his god Maha-deo, for whom he built a temple. He found pleasure in learning by heart the names of the thousand gods contained in the dictionary of the gods' names. He also taught me the chants and praises of the gods. I began to love and respect my brother for his great religiousness. I felt sure that such a zealous idol-worshipper would go to heaven, and that I too, somehow, by his merit, would reach Paradise.'

CHAPTER III.

FIRST CONTACT WITH CHRISTIANS.

IN the year 1827, Tulsi Paul heard of a Mission school having been opened at Goruckpore by the missionary, the late Rev. W. Wilkinson. His thirst for knowledge not having been satisfied, he made up his mind to become a pupil of that school, although by this time he had passed the years of his early youth, and was the father of a family. His people were very much against his going to a Christian school, and they tried their utmost to prevent him from his purpose.

He writes about that time: 'After trying my best to get money and leave from my household, and not succeeding, I washed my hands of my good name and my honour and pride, and, leaving my wife and my children and all I had, I went away secretly to Goruckpore. I was infatuated with the desire to obtain more knowledge, which would, I thought, open to me the mystery of truth; and this seemed to be worth many tears and privations and self-denials.'

After four days of travel, he reached Goruckpore, and found a caste brother who took him in, and provided for his wants. This man introduced him to two of the teachers of the Mission school. But Tulsi Paul, hearing the praises of Jay Narain's College in Benares, and of a rich man of his own caste who would certainly support him, he left Goruckpore without telling his friend, and in due time arrived there. To his great disappointment, he found that that rich caste brother would have nothing to say to him. Besides, cholera was raging in the town, and he found it necessary to stay over night outside the city. Greatly depressed by these untoward circumstances, he made up his mind to return home to his family.

When he reached Goruckpore, however, his caste brother was greatly surprised to see him, and asked, 'Why did you go away without letting us know? I wanted to introduce you to the missionary, and the two teachers were also inquiring after you.' He answered, 'Well, what is better than that you take me there now? What does a blind man want but two eyes? Is it not with the desire of acquiring knowledge that I am roaming about the whole world?'

Then Tulsi Paul goes on to tell of his first interview with the missionary, Mr. Wilkinson, and of his kindness in allowing him two rupees a month for his board, and giving him a room to live in, and thus enabling him to become a pupil of the Mission school.

This was not actually the first time in his life that Tulsi Paul had come into contact with Christians or Christianity. As a lad attending a religious fair, he was attracted by a crowd surrounding a preacher of the Gospel. Strange words fell on his ears: 'O generation of vipers!' Anxious to know what they could possibly mean, he listened with intense interest. However, he did not seem to have taken in the Gospel message, but the solemn words, 'O generation of vipers!' were never forgotten. They rang in his ears with increased solemnity as years went on, leaving him no peace or rest within.

Tulsi Paul felt very happy in the Mission school, and diligently pursued his studies. The school was opened with prayer by the missionary, followed by a Scripture lesson. Of the prayer he says: 'During the prayer I saw the whole assembly, whether Mohammedan or Hindu, each and every one bow their heads. Some bowed sincerely, and with devotion, whilst others did it hypocritically. I did not do so at first, because I had a feeling that as a Hindu I ought only to bow my head to the Supreme Being the Hindus acknowledge.'

Of the Mohammedan and Hindu teachers in the school he writes: 'Before the missionary they would agree with all he taught, but afterwards tell us to keep to our own religion, and to pursue the road we were on.'

On Sundays, Tulsi Paul had the privilege of attending a Sunday class held by Miss Bird for heathen lads and young men of the Mission school. He speaks in high terms of this lady, a sister of the judge of Goruckpore, who seemed to have taken a great interest in these youths, and who also was in the habit of visiting the ladies in the zenanas.

Tulsi Paul continued for about four years at Goruckpore, when his father, Mansa Ram, died, and his elder brother became master of the house and of the business. He came and fetched away Tulsi Paul to pay his respects to two rajahs, very likely on some business connected with their estates. Here Tulsi Paul seems to have borne witness to the religion of Jesus Christ, and of the truths contained in the Bible.

Then he returned home with his brother, and stayed a few months with his family; but he evidently was not happy amongst them, for he writes of that time: 'I heard nothing but reproaches from all sides. They taunted me, saying, "Tulsi Ram has eaten with the English, and become a Christian at Goruckpore."

'I used to deny this, saying, "It is not true. I have not yet become a Christian, and you are greatly mistaken if you think the English try to make you eat their food. They act only nobly and uprightly. For instance, Mr. Wilkinson loves me as if I were his son, yet he has never once asked me to eat of his food. He has procured books for me all the way from Calcutta, and supplied me with pen, ink, paper, and food, and such excellent teachers, as my own father, the great and famous Mansa Ram, could not have done. Oh, believe me, I am very grateful to the missionary, and shall never be able to repay him all my life. I want to go back to him; my heart is not happy here."'

And he did go back to Goruckpore, not with the intention of becoming again a pupil in the Mission school, but to try and earn his own livelihood.

As regards his state of mind towards Christianity and its doctrines, he writes: 'I greatly liked the teaching of the Bible. I began to study for myself the Old and New Testaments, and to commit portions of it to memory. Among other parts I learned by heart the Sermon on the Mount. I also read with great interest other Christian books; and all the Bible teaching found much place in my heart.'

Still, up to this time Tulsi Paul seems to have had no personal dealings with God. The truth that the Christians' God and Saviour was the only one for him also—a sinner needing an efficient Saviour—had not yet been brought home to him, though no doubt the Holy Spirit had begun His blessed work in his soul.

Mr. Wilkinson procured for Tulsi Paul a situation as

teacher of the Hindustani language with a gentleman named Lieutenant Monro. When the latter was transferred to Saugur he took Tulsi Paul along with him; but, being sent on to Lahore, he dismissed him at Saugur. He then became a teacher in a school for boys under the patronage of the Resident of that place, a Mr. Sullivan. He also mentions that the chaplain, Mr. Greenwood, took an interest in that school.

After some years, Tulsi Paul's elder brother came to Saugur, and, taking up his brother's work, sent him home. He remained there for some time, and then went to Lucknow in search of employment. Here he found a teachership in a school for soldiers' boys, very likely to teach them to read and write the Hindustani character. The New Testament seems to have been the book for the reading lesson, much to the delight of Tulsi Paul. The school was in charge of a Mr. Patten, who, as Tulsi Paul says, was considered a subordinate. This Christian gentleman showed great kindness towards Tulsi Paul and the boys in his school. He collected them in his house on Sundays and gave them a Scripture lesson, Tulsi Paul also attending and answering the questions the boys failed to do. Seeing Tulsi Paul's interest in Christianity and his knowledge of the Bible, Mr. Patten began to read with him the Bible and other Christian books; and thus the Gospel was once more brought to the notice of this searcher after truth.

CHAPTER IV.

SPIRITUAL CONFLICT.

BUT now God's blessed time had come,—a time of which Tulsi Paul says, 'But now the grace of the Lord and Saviour Jesus Christ began to shine upon me.'

Mr. Patten read a book with him, called *Abstract of Exhortations*. This book made a deep impression on him; so much so, he adds, that he could not help coming to the conclusion that, whatever the world might think, the Christian religion was, after all, a very good one; and he began to wonder how others too could not see the beauty of such teachings as were contained, for instance, in the Sermon on the Mount: again, how people could scoff at a religion with such pure and holy doctrines and precepts.

But these thoughts led to inward conflicts, of which Tulsi Paul writes: 'My heart condemned me, saying, "What have you, being a Hindu, to do with these things? You had better study your own religious books. If you remain a staunch Hindu, then, in the age of righteousness, you will have twenty-four incarnations, and three spiritual guides, and twelve saints to wait on you. And for you, too, a spotless and holy incarnation will appear. He will be born of a stainless virgin of the house of a Brahmin in the country Sinhal. Do not get your heart unsettled about these matters."'

In order to quiet his conscience, Tulsi Paul now tried to practise both religions, the Christian and the Hindu. He continued to read the Gospel, but also went back with redoubled energy to idolatry, and lived again the life of an ascetic. He says that both religions were fighting in his heart for victory; but he found the more he tried to keep to the practices of his old religion the more dissatisfied he felt. It was about this time that he met the Rev. Mr. Smith of Benares, and the Rev. Mr. Mather of Mirzapore, who had come on a visit to Lucknow. They had several conversations with him, and how deeply Tulsi Paul was impressed by them is seen from the fact that he remembered even the place (a certain well of some great man called Fath Ali) where he first met them, and he also relates part of the talks they had with him. Before parting, Mr. Smith said to Tulsi Paul, 'If you have doubts, and questions to be answered, do write to me to Benares, and I will always be ready to send you a reply.' Mr. Smith also gave him the book called *Investigation of True Religion*.

Of this book Tulsi Paul says: 'When I began to study this book all the conflicts in my heart began afresh, and in vain my old religion struggled against the new faith. I could not help seeing how all the incarnations and divinities of other religions were false and sinful, and that the only true, stainless, and perfect incarnation was the Lord God Jesus Christ.[1] I was overwhelmed at the thought of my caste, my religion, all my gods

---

[1] Mark how henceforth Tulsi Paul always calls our Lord 'the Lord God.'

and images and idols vanishing to nothing—nothing. My heart said to me, "Now is the time to decide whether you will choose God or keep to the world. Here is a plain question of giving up one thing and taking up another."

'I was so preoccupied with these doubts and perplexities, that I could not any more give proper attention to my daily work; and my superiors, after remonstrating with me several times, had to dismiss me. Then my family began to upbraid me. But oh, what could I do? And how could I give attention to all and everything? There those gentlemen were complaining of me, here my family were upbraiding me, and this heart of mine was also complaining and wanting to be attended to; and over and above all God was calling me to attend to Him. And I, I was only one, and could attend only to one thing first. And my heart said, "Choose the right thing." But how could I? I was in a great dilemma. I had lost my situation, and if I now became a Christian, would people not say, "Ah, his tree of support has been cut down, so he quickly becomes a Christian from secular motives"? I groaned in my spirit, saying, "O Lord God Jesus Christ, cast me not off! The world is trying to get hold of me, but Thou knowest the true state of my heart, for no secret is hid from Thee."

'After agonising thus in prayer, I felt greatly strengthened. Courage came into my heart, saying, "O Tulsi Ram, be not afraid! There is light to the strong and the brave." Blessed be the Lord God Jesus Christ for thus strengthening those whom He wishes to make His own! And then God, who alone can make a way out of every difficulty, began to make my way plain, by His guiding me to meet the Brigade-Major W. Lamb.'

Major Lamb took a great interest in his case. Tulsi

Paul opened his heart to him, and it was through his help that he found a situation in the Government College, under Mr. Martin, as record keeper. It is wonderful how many Christian gentlemen Tulsi Paul met in his career, who greatly helped him on in his search after truth. He mentions a Mr. Culling, the superintendent of his office, who, to his great joy and comfort, also read the Bible with him. Then Major Lamb had a Sunday class for his native servants and the officials; and he made use of Tulsi Paul to explain the Gospel story to them in the Hindustani language. Tulsi Paul did this in a way which left no doubt as to his being a Christian at heart; but when Major Lamb asked him why he did not seal his faith by baptism, he alleged several reasons, the chief one being that he hoped still to get his wife and children to join him.

CHAPTER V.

THE LORD JESUS GAINS THE VICTORY.

AFTER Tulsi Paul had been some time in Mr. Martin's office, Major Lamb informed him that his brother was coming out from England to be a missionary at Meerut. Tulsi Paul was greatly rejoiced at this piece of good news, for he felt that somehow his ardent desire would now be fulfilled, and that the missionary, whose brother he revered so greatly, would remove all doubts from his mind, and clear the path for him to accept Christ. He writes, he kept asking Major Lamb, 'Oh, when will the missionary come?' and would get the reply, 'Soon, soon; very soon.'

Tulsi Paul in his impatience asked Mr. Culling to allow him to resign his office, as he had quite made up his mind to attach himself to the missionary, Mr. Lamb.

Mr. Culling tried his best to induce Tulsi Paul to stay in his present situation, and at last he offered him an increase of pay. 'But,' writes Tulsi Paul, 'I thought within myself, "If I only get ten rupees a month, that will suffice for my wants. What do I care for the twenty-five rupees a month Mr. Culling is offering me? I do not care for money. Have I not spent large sums of my own, in order to find God and the truth? And if now I only succeed in getting the Lord God Jesus Christ, I get more than all riches. I am only longing for the comfort of being sure of having salvation."

'So, when Mr. Lamb arrived, I, Paul, left for good my children, my wife, my family pride, my caste, and, with a certificate of good conduct from the esteemed Mr. Culling, I went to Meerut with Mr. Lamb, who engaged me as teacher of the Hindustani language, for as yet the reverend gentleman did not know a word of it.

'When we arrived at Meerut, what was my astonishment to see that there too was a large and beautiful Mission school, under the Christian teacher, Inayat Masih, Mr. Rebsh being the head-master. The conclusion of it all was, that at last our Lord Jesus Christ gained the victory, and I, Paul, received baptism from Mr. Lamb in the same year, the year of our Lord 1847; and at the baptism I received the name "Paul." The name of Christ was then also put upon me [Masíhí, "Christian"]. It is to me a holy bequest and a strong protection. He in truth and verity is the Christ, the Light of the world, and this Lord Jesus is also my Light and my Refuge. I, Paul, believe this from my heart, and confess it here. Oh, believe on Him, my countrymen. Take up His easy yoke, and He will also show to you the way of life. Oh, kiss His blessed feet, and bow to Him, although you are not capable of grasping the depths of His wonderful being.

'It is commonly reported by outsiders that during the baptismal service the missionaries do, who knows what, to the converts—that they pour water into the mouth, or force them to eat beef.[1] But oh, the convert has

---

[1] Tulsi Paul confessed once, that often during his conflicts, when he had nearly made up his mind to be baptized, the dread of being forced to eat beef, again and again proved too strong an obstacle to surmount.

nothing of the kind to do. Christ's religion is not carnal, but spiritual, and has nothing to do with outward usages. I had searched and investigated this matter for twenty-four years before I became a Christian. Confess the Lord Jesus Christ, and believe that He is God, and that He became man in order to shed His blood as an atonement for sin, and this faith will be counted unto us for righteousness.

'When I, Paul, accepted Him who is the King of kings, the Lord of lords, the Prophet of prophets, and the great High Priest, I became His soldier, and received the weapons of warfare—the girdle of truth, the breastplate of righteousness, the sandals of the Gospel of peace, the shield of faith, the helmet of salvation, the sword of the Holy Spirit; and then, according to Christ's admonition, having put my hand to the plough, I did not look back again.'

CHAPTER VI.

TULSI PAUL PREACHES CHRIST.

TULSI PAUL, who was now a middle-aged man, became a happy and bright Christian, filled with love and zeal for his Lord. He was a man full of life and spirit and energy, quick in his movements and quick in his speech, and his keen eyes took in everything at a glance. He was upright and sincere, a man in whom was no guile; somewhat eccentric, and very original; fond of quoting proverbs, passages from books, and very fond of speaking in rhymed sentences, which came quite naturally to him. His affable manners, true Oriental politeness, his simplicity and humility, won the hearts of all with whom he came in contact.

He was a fine-looking man, tall and slender, with a noble aristocratic bearing. He kept strictly to his native costume and native food, and was scrupulously clean in his dress and person. He was very abstemious. His chief food consisted of *chupatties* and *dal* (unleavened bread and pulse). He denied himself all luxuries, even the *hukkah*.[1] The only indulgence he allowed himself was tea, and that he discontinued for a time, when he found he was getting too much addicted to it.

---

[1] Indian pipe.

After his baptism he began at once to preach Christ; but the blasphemous way in which many Mohammedan opponents argued with him touched him to the quick, and he often gave vent to his indignation, and answered angrily. But on being shown by his friend, the Rev. Mr. Lamb, that this was not the spirit of the meek and lowly Jesus, he strove to conquer his temper, and God gave him the victory over it. It is said that in later years, on more than one occasion, some scoffer in the crowd would fill his shoe with stones and throw it at the preacher, upon which he would simply turn round to see who had insulted him, and quietly go on preaching.

Once, when this was done while he was walking home from addressing the people in company with a lad who carried his books, the latter heard him repeating to himself, ' " The servant is not greater than his Master; if they have persecuted Me, they will also persecute you." Yes, Jesus my Lord has said, " Whosoever will smite thee on thy right cheek, turn to him the other also. Love your enemies, bless them that curse you, do good to them that hate you, and pray for them that despitefully use you, and persecute you." '

For ten years, from 1847 to 1857, Tulsi Paul worked uninterruptedly under Mr. Lamb's guidance, faithfully and zealously preaching the Word, itinerating a good part of each year in the North-West Provinces, in the district of Meerut, and along the banks of the Ganges. The seed sown thus bore abundant fruit, for it was from the latter districts that the nucleus of the Annfield congregation was gathered, of which Tulsi Paul became the first pastor.

The memorable year of the Mutiny, 1857, dawned as peacefully as any of its predecessors had done. Early in the year, Mr. Lamb and his family, with Tulsi Paul, set out on their annual tour to the Hurdwar fair, little dreaming of the awful tragedies that were so soon to be enacted in that neighbourhood. Their march extended through the Eastern Doon to Dehra, and from there to Landour, a town on the Himalaya hills. Here Mr. Lamb left his family, and, accompanied by Tulsi Paul, marched on into the interior, towards the independent State of Teeree.

In the meantime the Mutiny broke out in Meerut, on May 10, 1857, and rumours of it soon reached Mr. Lamb. He at once returned to Landour to his family. But even then he would not give up speaking and preaching in the bazaar, although the natives became very turbulent and restless; and Major Rind, a staunch friend of his, apprehended that some harm might be done to Christ's faithful messenger. He therefore urged him to leave his wife and children in his care, and go back into the interior, where he could with less danger pursue the Lord's work, as the State of Teeree was loyal to the English.

Mr. Lamb agreed to this plan, and on June 7, 1857, while riding back from Major Rind's house, after arranging final matters with him on the subject of his journey, his horse shied at a pony carrying *pakháls*,[1] backed, and went over the precipice. Mr. Lamb was thrown on the Waverley Road, some forty feet below, and in about thirty-six hours died from the injuries he had sustained.

This was a great blow to Tulsi Paul, for he was deeply attached to Mr. Lamb, and he grieved long for him. He stayed on with Mrs. Lamb for that year, and worked under her direction, conducting services for the native Christians, and otherwise making himself useful in the Lord's work.

[1] Leather bags filled with water.

Long after the actual Mutiny was quelled, the natives remained in a very disturbed state; but, fearless of consequences, Tulsi Paul was about his Father's business, and took every opportunity of preaching in the bazaars. On one occasion, while proclaiming the Gospel message in some public place, an English officer rode up to him, and told him to stop preaching. He also ordered him to pay a fine for disobeying orders. Tulsi Paul paid the fine, rather a large sum; but the very next day found him at his post as usual. The officer again got information, and, riding up, said, 'Did I not forbid you to preach? You preachers and native Christians are at the bottom of the Mutiny, and would you again bring us such trouble? Leave off this preaching, and let me never see you here again.'

'O no,' said the preacher, 'I am not preaching mutiny, but peace—the Gospel message of peace. And I am telling the people how wrong it is to have wars and fightings.'

The officer either did not understand him, or he was put out at his venturing to remonstrate with him. He suddenly rode up and struck Christ's messenger with his whip across the face, and forced him to leave the place.

It was touching to hear Tulsi Paul alluding to this event in later years, excusing the officer by putting down his conduct more to his ignorance than to any ill feeling. But as the heart rises in indignation at such treatment of a Gospel preacher, another scene arises which speaks, 'Peace, be still,' to the angry billows of indignation,—for Tulsi Paul was privileged to pay back this act in Christian coin to another of Her Majesty's army. A British soldier lay dying in the Meerut hospital. He was longing before his departure once more to eat the bread and drink the cup of the Lord, in remembrance of Him; but there was no one to give it to him—the chaplain was ill, and the missionary absent. A happy thought occurred to some friend, who went and fetched Tulsi Paul, then pastor in Maliyana; and he gladly did what was required.

It was far from Tulsi Paul's intention to defy Government. He was a most loyal subject, and always spoke in the highest terms of British rule in India, and of the benefits derived from it.

CHAPTER VII.

TULSI PAUL'S GREAT TRIAL.

THE great trial of Tulsi Paul's life was, that neither his wife nor his children followed him in his faith. Long did he cherish the hope of welcoming at least some of his family into the fold of Jesus. But to this man, whom God had chosen to be the instrument of bringing many heathen and outsiders into the kingdom of Christ, was not given the joy of gathering in some sheaves from his own house and family.

He visited them as often as he was able, and spoke to them of the only way to everlasting life; but all his endeavours seemed in vain. His wife especially was very bitter against him, and whenever he came she had nothing but hard words and abuse for him, calling him an outcast and a disgrace to his family, and saying that he had only become a Christian in order to suck cows' bones. Tulsi Paul did not retaliate; he listened most patiently and meekly to all her insults, hoping in the end to win her over.

Tulsi Paul had two daughters, beautiful fair girls. They were named Sonee and Monee, and their father was deeply attached to them. He sometimes took presents and gay garments for them, and tried to induce them to come near him; but their mother would not allow them to approach, and all he was permitted to do was to feast his eyes on them from a distance. Perhaps it was this that made him so tender towards other little girls. He never passed any of his congregation without taking some notice of them, generally saying, 'Well, *betiyá*,'[1] or *lalí*,[2] 'and are you quite well?'

He had also two sons. Later on, his younger son, together with his wife, did accept baptism; but he was only a nominal Christian, and no one seems to know what really induced him to leave Hinduism. He was not a good man, and was a source of great grief to his father. However, on this son's death-bed, Tulsi Paul had the comfort of being with him, and seeing him truly penitent, and dying in true faith in Him who came to save sinners.

Tulsi Paul had great compassion on the young widow left by this son. He regularly paid her ten rupees a month for her support, which was about a fourth part of his whole income. However, he had only to do so for two years, after which she married again.

But all the father's hopes were centred in his first-born son, Ayudhiya Prashad, who was his favourite; and nothing could lessen his love for him, or shake his fervent hope of his ultimate conversion. Even with his dying breath he besought this son to confess the Lord.

Ayudhiya seemed to love his father, and showed true filial attachment to him. He often visited him, and stayed with him for longer or shorter periods. But although he pretended to be one with him in mind, and would even prepare his father's food, he himself

---

[1] Pet name for a daughter. [2] Little damsel.

would not eat a morsel of bread which his father had touched.

Ayudhiya Prashad had a remarkably good knowledge of the truths of Christianity. Often, too, he seemed to be almost persuaded to be baptized, but he put it off again and again, waiting for a more convenient season; but that season never came. He died some twenty years after his father, and was up to the very last a teacher employed by the Rev. H. Stern of Goruckpore, who often spoke to him very seriously of thus hardening his heart. His last excuse was that he could not break his old mother's heart by giving up his caste, and that he would wait till she died, and then take the final step. But Ayudhiya Prashad did not reckon that the call would come to him before it came to his mother. He was only ill a few days, dying rather suddenly, and quite unexpectedly.

The state of his family was a great and sore trial to the faith of good Tulsi Paul; and now and then, with tears in his eyes, he would pour out his heart on this subject to his missionary friends, and wonder why the Lord did not answer his prayers and supplications for his beloved ones.

In the beginning of the year 1858, Tulsi Paul left Mrs. Lamb and went to Agra, to be prepared for ordination; and in the following year he was ordained by Bishop Cotton, together with the Rev. David Mohan of Allahabad, and others. The bishop wished to give each of the candidates a memento of this occasion, and allowed them to choose what they would have. One chose a watch, and Tulsi Paul was asked if he would like one too. His answer was most characteristic: 'O no, I need no watch; my watch is in the sky.' He asked for a reference Bible in Urdu; but as such a thing was not to be had in those days, an English one was given him, which, however, he could not use, as he did not know English.

After his ordination he was appointed pastor of the Annfield Church. The congregation there had been gathered together and organised into a Christian colony by Major Rind. They were converts from among the Hindu agriculturists round about the Meerut district, who had heard the truth from Mr. Lamb and Tulsi Paul, and embraced Christianity. In those days native Christians were much more persecuted than they are now, and it was generally believed to be almost impossible for converts to remain in their own villages.

When after his ordination the Rev. Tulsi Paul arrived in Annfield, it was late at night. He had walked twenty-two miles from Dehra, with only a Christian lad carrying his baggage. No foolish pride in his new position influenced him, and he lived the same simple life as pastor that he had as catechist. The two belated travellers lost their way in the dark, and stood shouting across the stream near Major Rind's house, not finding the place for crossing. Major Rind sent his servants with a lantern to show them the way, and received the new pastor very heartily, putting him up for the night.

Major Rind greatly honoured and respected Tulsi Paul, in whom he found the right man for the work before him —that of building up a church then in its infancy. And although at times he might be a little too outspoken and impetuous with his superiors, Major Rind knew the sincerity and uprightness which called forth such plain speaking of what the pastor considered the right thing, and bore with it. He often invited him to his house, and treated him as an honoured guest and a personal friend. He loved to speak of him as his private chaplain.

He was always asked to conduct family prayers and ask a blessing at meals, and this in the Hindustani language, as he did not know English. And Mrs. Rind, in kind thoughtfulness, knowing that her guest did not care for English food, had always prepared for him the native dishes she knew he liked. He kept to the native custom of eating with his fingers, but he did it in so refined a manner that no offence could be taken. Tulsi Paul was also a great friend of Major Rind's children; he listened most patiently to their childish prattle, and joined in all their little interests; and his good advice and counsel to them, given in his own quaint way, was not forgotten by them.

CHAPTER VIII.

TULSI PAUL'S WORK AS PASTOR.

THE Rev. Tulsi Paul's introduction to his new flock was a very happy occasion. Most of the people had known him in former years, and had first heard the message of salvation through Christ from his lips. They remembered the time when, in their heathen homes, this good man had come to them and told them of the loving Saviour, and how gladly they had listened to the message of free pardon and forgiveness, and at last accepted the truth; and now they had the joy of welcoming him among them as their future pastor and friend. And as to the new pastor, he came to them full of love and zeal, willing to spend and be spent for the good of their souls.

One of his first undertakings was the building of a temporary church. Major Rind and other Christian friends helped him, and he soon had a place for worship, a schoolhouse, and a small house for himself ready. And then he turned his attention to the spiritual wants of his congregation, and endeavoured to help the members to walk worthy of the vocation wherewith they were called; for as yet some of them were only 'babes in

Christ,' and needed careful nurturing, and others were but nominal Christians, who had joined the new faith with not the purest motives.

He visited his people regularly from house to house, and by showing sympathy with them in all their various difficulties and troubles, and helping them, too, as best he could, he kept in touch with them, and won their love and respect. He always conducted morning and evening prayers with the villagers, generally in the open air. If any quarrel arose, he would call upon the offending parties at these meetings, and ask them publicly to confess their fault, and beg forgiveness of each other. At other times he would get the disputants together privately, and exhort them and pray for them, and thus heal up the breach.

His modes of punishing delinquents were sometimes rather striking. One punishment for a man who had offended was to kneel down, take off his turban, and balance a large stone on his head for some time! If any one had been guilty of using bad language, he would have to carry a heavy stone on his head, and go from house to house, wherever his abusive words had been heard, and ask for forgiveness.

As to hardened characters, the pastor would adhere to the Scripture method. First, he would reason with them. If this proved unavailing, he would send two or three of their friends to talk to them. If this too failed, he would take witnesses with him, and say to the offender, 'I spoke to you alone, and you did not listen; I sent your friends to you, and you did not mind; I now come with two or three witnesses to beseech you to repent; but if you still persist in your wrong-doing, know that henceforth you shall be to us as a heathen and a publican. I deliver you to Satan for the destruction of the flesh, and pray that your spirit may be saved.' After this he would take no more notice of the offending parties. This treatment saved many a man from persisting in his evil course.

The pastor urged very particularly regular attendance at church. His sermons were practical and to the point, and he did not shirk disagreeable topics, not being at all given to please his listeners by speaking to them 'smooth things.' He also made frequent use of very homely similes. Once he greatly shocked an English lady by comparing 'faith' to a *jháran* (duster, or dish-cloth). She could not help remonstrating with him, in pious indignation, about using this extraordinary simile for such a lofty subject. But the simple-minded preacher could not see at all that he had done anything improper. He took the trouble of reiterating his whole sermon before his lady judge, trying to show her how faith was indeed a *jháran*, cleaning and removing the stains of unbelief, superstition, sin; and by the help of which we escape unhurt from Satan's hot and burning designs.

The pastor would brook no inattention during his sermons; but, as he was in the habit of preaching very long discourses, it was sometimes hard on the poor tired cultivators. But, nevertheless, woe to him who chanced to fall asleep! Suddenly, in the middle of the sermon, there would be an ominous pause, and then three loud claps on the pulpit. If this did not arouse the sleeper, the preacher would call out his name and ask him to come forward, and then quietly go on with his sermon, leaving the unfortunate man standing till it was over. It was very difficult for the rest of the congregation to keep serious during such a scene, especially when, on one occasion during harvest-time, three such delinquents were made to come forward. Not often, however, was such a sore punishment needed; the fear of it kept many a sleepy eye wide open.

Still, as the pastor continued to preach such very long sermons, the congregation at last ventured to remonstrate. They sent a deputation to him, to state how greatly they appreciated his love for them and his sincere interest in their spiritual welfare, but that they would beg of him to make his sermons somewhat shorter, as they could not fix their attention for such a length of time.

No false pride prevented the pastor from taking this hint to heart, and he promised to reform. When the deputation had left, he called Stephen, a Christian lad of whom he was very fond, and whom he kept as a kind of servant and companion, and told him to listen well to his sermons, and when he thought they were getting too long, just to stand up for a moment. This should be a sign between them; 'for,' added the zealous preacher simply, 'when I am preaching I forget all about time and everything else, and certainly I must not go on till they can listen no longer.'

Stephen did not at all like this task, and yet, after a few Sundays, when once his master forgot his promise to his congregation, and preached on and on, and Stephen's neighbours began to push him and sign to him, he had to do it. Most awkwardly did he rise up for a moment, and then quickly sat down again, looking very bashful and uncomfortable.

The Rev. Tulsi Paul won the respect of his people to a remarkable degree. They submitted cheerfully to his authority, and obeyed him implicitly; but they not only reverenced him, they also loved him. They said he was so sympathetic and loving, and a real and true friend and comforter to all who were in need or distress. When he visited the poor of his flock, he paid them as much honour, and was as polite to them, as to any of his rich members; and he would sit down and eat as hearty a meal of their coarse, simple fare as he would of a sumptuous feast prepared by a rich neighbour.

If any of his members were ill, he would visit them daily, administering spiritual food and medicine, and also caring for the poor suffering bodies. Any little comforts, such as milk, sugar, tea, and other things, which he thought they could not afford to buy, he would provide them with out of his own pocket. To this day the older members of the Annfield congregation remember these beautiful traits in their beloved first pastor. Indeed, he was often *too* generous with his money, and at times became involved in difficulties. Eventually he gave his money to Mrs. Lamb or Mrs. Rind to keep for him, feeling it was safer with them; but even then he was constantly drawing from them and giving away. And what he gave he always gave most cheerfully; it was a real pleasure to him to do so. He often used to say, 'God gave me this money, and I give it Him back in this way;' or, 'There, take it; I have no one who needs it;' adding sadly, 'I have no wife, no children, to leave it to. They are no more mine; they are of the world, and the world gives them all they need. You are my children, whom the Lord has given me.'

Some years later, good Tulsi Paul began to save up his money in real earnest. He formed some idea of buying up land, and settling poor native Christians on it, making himself responsible for the rent; his tender heart was torn with pity for those poor Christians who found it very difficult at times to pay up land rents. And he had some idea that after his death this land should go to the Mission, and be kept on with the same object. This well-meant but unpractical plan did not mature, and at his death he bequeathed his savings—500 rupees—to the Goruckpore Mission, where he spent his last two years.

But his pastoral work at Annfield was not all plain sailing. Several of the Christians had been polygamists in their heathen days. When the Annfield colony was organised, and Christian rules enforced, the converts were asked to keep only one wife; but some of them tried to evade this rule, by sometimes having one wife with them, and by and by sending her away to her village, and substituting another for her. The ever-watchful eye of their pastor soon detected this evil, and he tried to put a stop to such proceedings. First, he reasoned with them, trying to show them their wrong-doing; but when they persisted in their conduct, and every other measure failed, they had to be expelled from the colony. They joined another Mission, and revenged themselves by forming a conspiracy which very nearly ruined their pastor's reputation. They spread untrue reports about him, charging him also with the most heinous sins. Petitions were even presented to the bishop, who was then on a tour of visitation in the Doon. The bishop felt them to be so serious that he instituted a legal inquiry into the whole case, and had all the charges thoroughly gone through before competent judges.

The congregation at Annfield was filled with indignation at their pastor being so maligned, and wanted to go *en masse* and stand up for him and his innocence; but twenty men only were allowed to present themselves. The result of the inquiry was a complete acquittal of the accused. The bishop was so convinced of his innocence, that with his own hand he wrote him an Urdu letter exonerating him from all blame.

All this was a great trial to the sensitive nature of

this good man. Few knew how keenly he felt it. What was specially humiliating was, that some of the European judges seemed to believe the report. Years after, when he once unburdened his heart to a missionary on this subject, he was still grieving over it, and said with tears, 'Oh, how could English gentlemen, English Christian men, even for a moment think of a pastor, a Christian religious teacher, acting thus ? And when I was acquitted, why did not one of them come forward and shake hands with me, and thus show that they believed me to be innocent ? Did they still doubt me ? God only knows what I suffered at that time !'

CHAPTER IX.

TULSI PAUL'S DISCIPLES, AND HIS PREACHING TOURS.

FOR some time the Rev. Tulsi Paul acted as headmaster of the Annfield Boys' School, but it did not prosper under his management. One reason may have been that he was so absorbed in the interest of the 'one thing needful,' that whatever the subject of the lesson he had to give might be, it invariably ended in a Bible lesson, and the boys did not get on with their secular studies.

He had not much sympathy with boys playing,—he called it wasting time,—and he had an especial dislike to their flying kites for hours together. He would remind them of the preciousness of time, saying, 'Time is precious, time is fleeting. Do not fritter away your days in play and nonsense. Go and do something useful, or take your books and study.'

Once, on account of excessive heat, the boys of a Christian school were given a holiday. About noon a native juggler happened to come to the premises, and the boys begged their superintendent, a young missionary lately come from England, to allow the juggler to show off his tricks. Leave was granted, and soon they all sat

INDIAN JUGGLERS.

down in a circle, watching the wonderful feats of an Indian juggler.

Suddenly, in the midst of the performance, the old pastor was seen running towards them in great excitement, in half undress, his flowing robes blown about in the high wind, without even his turban to protect his head from the burning mid-day sun. Rushing into the room of the superintendent, and forgetting his usual politeness, he flung about his arms, and called out excitedly, 'Oh, *sahib* [sir], what are you doing? what are you doing? Oh, stop that business outside! We are here to preach against the devil and all his works, and you, a missionary, allow it to be carried on at your very doors!'

The young missionary tried to expostulate with the old man, and to explain that deftness of hands and not devil's play was the secret here; but the pastor would not be convinced.

'No, no,' he cried out; 'you do not understand. I have seen a good deal of this kind of thing. Oh, for God's sake, stop that business!'

The missionary went out and sent away the juggler.

The pastor, while in Annfield, took, however, an especial interest in young men, and he chose twelve from his congregation to be his chosen pupils. These he called his 'twelve disciples,' adding, with a pleasant smile, 'The Lord Jesus chose twelve, and taught them in a special manner; I will do the same.'

He kept these young men constantly about him, and taught and influenced them personally. As being so much with him prevented often their earning money elsewhere, he now and then gave them presents of food and clothing. When giving them anything, he would generally say, 'Take this, and be thankful to God, and always keep in mind that it is He who provides you with all things needful.'

His treatment of them was a little eccentric at times. Stephen, the lad mentioned above, was one of the twelve. One night the pastor suddenly woke up this youth, and asked him, 'Stephen, Stephen, who made the stars?'

Stupefied with sleep, the lad growled out, 'How do I know?'

'What!' called out his master, in a tone which thoroughly aroused the lad, 'you do not know who made the stars? Get up at once, and go outside and look at them, till you remember who their Maker is.'

The young fellow went out meekly and humbly; and while he stood outside his master went on: 'My son, sleeping or waking, you ought always to remember the Lord. Let Him become a part of your being, and then even in your sleep you will remember Him.'

The lad Stephen never forgot that night's lesson.

This youth was paid one anna and a half daily, for which he had to work hard. If he seemed inclined to grumble, his master would say to him, 'My son, do not despise the day of small things. I am a *zemíndár's* [land-owner's] son, and yet I had only two rupees a month when I first left home. Whatever you have, learn to live on it, and try to save something too.'

One of those very disciples afterwards acknowledged that following this advice had made him a rich man.

The Rev. Tulsi Paul was in every sense of the word a man of prayer; and while thus engaged he loved to address his 'Lord God' in high Arabic words. Sometimes, however, the thought would perhaps occur to him that he was speaking before these simple agriculturists in an unknown tongue, and he would interpret immediately after, and use a homely Hindustani word. This was disturbing, and sometimes had a ludicrous effect; but the speaker evidently did it unconsciously.

There was a saying among his congregation, that their pastor was so holy he needed almost no sleep; for, whatever time at night he was wanted, he was found awake, sitting on his bed, wrapped in his large native shawl, reading, praying, or meditating; and the first rays of sunlight saw him again at his devotions. Even when he was a catechist, Mr. Lamb often remonstrated with him for keeping up half the night to read and study the Bible, fearing his health would suffer; but it really did seem that Tulsi Paul needed less sleep than others. Do we not find in these hours of communion with the Lord, the secret of the holy and consistent life of this servant of Christ?

On one occasion the child of one of his disciples fell suddenly ill. Though it was the middle of the night, the father rushed off to his pastor, sure of help from him. He found him as usual sitting up in bed meditating, with his Bible open before him. After listening with sympathy to the tale of sorrow, the good man said, 'My son, I have no medicine for your child, nor can I get any at this time of night. But I have one remedy at hand—prayer. I will come with you, and use that.'

On the road the pastor stumbled over a stone, and fell. The father of the child was full of concern; but the man of God got up quickly, and begged his pardon for causing him pain by his carelessness, and walked on. Arriving at the house, he comforted the parents, and prayed for the sick one. Prayer prevailed, and the child recovered.

Whenever the Rev. Tulsi Paul went on preaching tours, he always took several of his young men with him. They had to carry the books and tracts, their blankets, etc. When they stopped to preach, one of them had to stand up and read a passage of Scripture, and then, when the crowd was gathered, Tulsi Paul would preach to them. In his younger days he always walked these tours, but when age began to tell on him he was urged to buy a small country pony. He consented with great reluctance, and at first hardly ever rode on it. Sometimes, when his young disciples would try to induce him to ride, he would say, 'No, children; you are walking, why should I ride?' When at last he was very tired, he would in a manner apologise for his conduct, saying, 'Now you must forgive an old man, but I cannot walk any longer.'

And as years went on, and strength declined more and more, the good old man had to give up all walking, and then he was always seen on his pony going to or returning from his work. And, strange to say, his groom was a Brahmin. It is a very rare thing indeed to see a man of this caste take to this work, but the man seemed to be so deeply attached to his master, that, rather than leave him, he attended also the pony, besides being cook and general servant.

The Rev. Tulsi Paul was up to the very last a most indefatigable bazaar preacher, and he always made it a point to visit as many religious fairs for the same purpose as he had time and opportunity. During these fairs he would hardly allow himself time for his meals.

Sometimes the audience would call out, 'Tell us something new; you always speak of Jesus Christ. We are tired of hearing about Him.'

'Tired of hearing about the Lord Christ?' the preacher would say, a beautiful expression lighting up his face. 'I am never tired of hearing or talking about my Lord, the Saviour of the world. Take from me my wife, take from me my children, take my lands and my money, take everything, yea, even life itself, but leave me Christ in my heart!

He was very much interested in all Hindu Faqírs and devotees. When once he began to talk to them, it was difficult to get him away. 'Yes, yes, I am coming,' he would say to those who urged the tired preacher to come away; but again and again would he turn to his listeners, and try to show them the beauty of that religion which offers salvation, a present salvation, free, without money and without price. He would point out clearly to them how impossible it was for sinners to earn salvation by the penances and tortures they inflicted upon themselves, and how all their meritorious deeds and religious acts were dead works, and could not be acceptable to a holy and righteous God.

In those days there were few printed *bhajans* (native hymns set to native tunes), but the Rev. Tulsi Paul had the gift of composing them on the spur of the moment, and he sang them to the listening crowds, drawing thus great numbers, to whom he then preached the Word. One of the hymns he composed was a very long one, each line beginning with a letter of the Hindi alphabet.

He was permitted to carry on his work at Annfield till the year 1866, but then, with the steady growth of the colony, his pastoral duties became too heavy for him, and he was transferred to Maliyana and Kankarkhera, outstations of Meerut. He stayed there for only two years, and wrote his autobiography. It may be that thus recalling his past life, and in spirit living it over again, stirred up the great yearning he began to have to go back to the neighbourhood of his home and family, in order, if possible, to influence them; for it was at his own urgent wish that he was transferred to Goruckpore, and put in charge of the native Christian congregation at Basharatpore.

CHAPTER X.

TULSI PAUL'S LAST YEARS AND DEATH.

THE last two years of his life were spent at Basharatpore. Every one in the Christian village soon began to respect and revere the old, venerable-looking pastor, who, notwithstanding his age and infirmity, took a personal interest in them and in all their affairs, and could help them not only in spiritual matters, but also advise them (having been a *zemindár's* son) in questions about their fields, their cattle, and their crops.

In the afternoon he would often ride into the town, and preach in the bazaars to Hindus and Mohammedans. It was a treat to see the venerable old man, with flowing white beard and flowing garments, gesticulating and waxing eloquent about his Lord God Jesus Christ, whom he urged his hearers to receive as their Saviour. He endured their abuse and scoffings most patiently, and had great tact in quieting down the tumult which they raised in order to get rid of him and his earnest preaching.

At last his health gave way, and he was laid up for months with dyspepsia. His favourite son, Ayudhiya Prashad, came at his request to nurse him, and to be with him. During his lingering and painful illness he was most patient, and full of faith and hope to the last.

The Word of God was his great comfort, and when his strength began to fail, his son had to read it out to him. The eighth chapter of the Epistle to the Romans was his favourite chapter, and as in his sermons he had frequently pointed out the preciousness of the words, 'We are children of God; and if children, then heirs, heirs of God, and joint-heirs with Christ,' so now on his death-bed he was fully conscious that all his sufferings, past and present, were not worthy to be compared with the glory which would be revealed.

One night, when he was already so weak that he could not move without being helped, he startled his son by suddenly sitting up in bed without any assistance, and, pointing up, said aloud, 'They are calling me.' His son tried to persuade him to lie down; but the old man, looking up, exclaimed again, 'I see a throne; the Lord is calling me!' Then Ayudhiya Prashad knew that his father's end had come, and, sobbing out in his grief, he said, 'Father, father! are you going to leave me? Shall I never see you again?' The dying man replied, 'Never, my son, unless you accept Christ. Will you not promise me, before my departure, to accept the Lord?' The son promised at that solemn moment that he would do so.

Tulsi Paul looked up again, and, lifting up his arms, he shouted out, 'Main átá hún! *K*hushí! *k*hushí!' [I am coming! Joy! joy!]

His body fell back on the pillows, and his spirit entered triumphantly into the joy of his Lord.

The next day, February 10, 1870, his remains were laid in the Goruckpore cemetery, to await the resurrection call of his Lord.

The Rev. H. Stern, when leaving the cemetery, said to the sorrowing flock of the late pastor, 'He was a true Israelite, in whom there was no guile.'

Besides the Christians from Goruckpore and Basharatpore, crowds of non-Christians had come to witness the funeral.

When leaving the graveyard, one of the Mohammedan *moulvies* was asked by the missionary what had brought him there, as the missionary had seen how on several occasions this very *moulvie* had shaken his fist in the face of the deceased preacher, when the latter used to proclaim Christ in the market-place.

'What brought me here?' was the sharp reply. 'Why, was he [Rev. Tulsi Paul] not a true servant of Allah?'

His Hindu wife, on hearing of the death of her husband, had an image of clay made, and burnt it, performing all the funeral rites according to her religion. And as regards Ayudhiya Prashad, he did not redeem the promise made to his father on his deathbed.

But though Tulsi Paul did not see the members of his family turning to the Lord, no doubt he will have found many other souls in Paradise his spiritual children, whom God, by his instrumentality, had gathered in to be of those who had washed their robes and made them white in the blood of the Lamb; and Tulsi Paul's joy is now full in being with Him whom having not seen he loved, because He had first loved him and called him out of darkness into His marvellous light.

> 'When Thy blood-bought Church, Lord Jesus
>   Is complete;
> When each soul is safely landed
>   At Thy feet;
> What a story, In the glory,
>   She'll repeat!'

www.ingramcontent.com/pod-product-compliance
Lightning Source LLC
Chambersburg PA
CBHW020827190426
43197CB00037B/726